ISBN: 978 0 9554100 62

'What is the soup of the day?' A short guide to understanding consumer behaviour in veterinary practice is a publication of Roman House Publishers.

Roman House
Ripon HG4 1LE
United Kingdom

www.vetstakecare.com

"What is the soup of the day?"

A short guide to understanding consumer behaviour – in veterinary practice

Ross Tiffin

Foreword

If this book itself were 'the soup of the day', it would be difficult for the waiter or waitress to describe. It is a very satisfying, hearty soup that is hard to put down and, once finished, leaves you wanting more. Like a clam chowder, it has an overall rich and satisfying consistency, with interesting ingredients. Some of those ingredients are familiar, others not. Some are recognisable and comforting, but to be honest others are unrecognisable and have a strange, dare I say it, unpalatable taste. Maybe it is an acquired taste, but it must all be assimilated and digested.

It is a nourishing soup in that it provides you with the building blocks to grow, but they aren't handed to you on a plate. There is work to be done. It is food for the brain. It provides many answers, but it also poses many questions, both for our industry and for us as individual businesses. The only constant is change, and we live in a time where the rate of change is exponential. As veterinarians we spend too much time looking into our soup for answers, the soup we have always ordered, stirring it occasionally to see what rises to the top. Not unexpectedly, it tends to be the same old ingredients, which we do little or nothing about, except perhaps watch them sink back into the murky depths.

In his book, Ross encourages us to take the recipe book off the shelf. No, he encourages us to get off our backsides, to go out and buy a new cookbook, maybe even one written by Heston Blumenthal, and to have the courage to cook up a new soup, a refined consommé perhaps or a tom yam that is more suited to today's diners.

Geoff Little MVB MRCVS
Veterinary Business Adviser
Anval Ltd

Contents

CHAPTER I
Introduction

Introduction

One of the most rewarding games to play is to ask your waiter or waitress 'What is the soup of the day?' In so many cases, no one seems to know. It's as if having a soup of the day is a tick-box commitment, something that's expected but usually not reflective of the restaurant's (or the Chef's) ambitions. Accordingly, it rarely filters down to the hapless waiting staff who, in turn, fail or forget to find out for themselves. Because so few people order it, it often goes undiscovered for days!

'There's nothing so queer as folk!' My grandmother was a canny Scot, and this was one of her favourite sayings. Subsequently, life has taught me that she was entirely right. Not only is it sometimes difficult to understand what people are saying, let alone thinking; it is very often hard to accept the logic of other people's point of view.

How often have you heard, or actually said, 'Which planet are they on, for heaven's sake? Don't they know that ... etc., etc?'

It is both a blessing and a disaster that people are different from one another. On a one-to-one basis, how could we find our partners and friends if everyone were the same? On a macro basis, however, how on earth are we going to conduct business when everyone needs to be treated as an individual? In reality, of course, everyone **is** different – all 60 million of us in the UK – and it is only for convenience that we seek to pigeonhole people, using devices as varied as astrological star signs and social descriptors such as 'yuppies', 'dinkies', 'chavs' and myriad others. While these are often just phrases of the moment, the constant reinvention of social grouping terminology illustrates our need to find ways of dividing up the galaxy of the population into easily recognisable sections. Some are more tangible, such as age, gender, creed or nationality, while others, such as those which reflect wealth or social standing, are far more difficult to operate in any reproducible form, despite the socio-economic tools that have been designed to assist us.

socio-economic groups When economists talk about people belonging to *socio-economic groups* labelled A, B, C1, C2 or D, this is often only meaningful within the esoteric world of researchers in this field and is often abused when taken out of context. As an example, category A is meant to denote people of high social standing, education and professional achievement, such as doctors, and with this comes the assumption that these people will have high net financial worth. As you move down the scale through B and C1 to C2 and D, the assumption is that people in these groups are less well educated or trained, are progressively more working class and will have a significantly lower disposable income. Yet, although in today's world people take early retirement from a myriad of jobs, may have index-linked pensions and even significant savings and may well enjoy a high disposable income, pensioners are still categorised as group D.

Similarly, in the 1950s tradesmen such as plumbers, electricians and plasterers would have been categorised as being in group C2, but in today's world many self-employed tradesmen have very high earning potential and a high disposable income, live in beautiful houses and send their children to private schools. The lesson to be remembered is to avoid the temptation to categorise people into convenient groups!

As an individual, how would you like to be treated?

■ What about respect, with appropriate recognition of your age, experience and social standing? Of course, we'd all like that, wouldn't we?

■ What about some acknowledgement that your time is precious? Perhaps.

■ What about some understanding that you either have or perhaps have not some experience of the situation you're discussing, or that you belong to a particular group, whether ethnic, religious or political? For some of us, these things are very important, and in certain situations this understanding will be critical to the successful outcome of any meeting or discussion.

Do you prefer to be addressed by your first name or by your surname with the prefix of Mr, Mrs or Ms? Some people hate the term Ms and prefer Miss; others find Miss to be old-fashioned.

Many who have striven to achieve academic or social honours are able to style themselves Dr, Professor, the Reverend, Major or even Sir or Lord. Having worked hard to achieve these prefixes, many people are insistent on others' recognition of them, while a different sector of the public might consider this pretentious outside any professional encounter.

How do you feel about music? For some, it cannot be considered music unless it has a discernable melody, while others prefer a techno-beat to rattle the dentition. When you listen, second hand, to other people's music on the train, does it irritate you or soothe you?

personal space Over and above all these social considerations, we have the phenomenon of body language. In the UK, we are rather keen to establish and protect a small area of space around us – we call it our *'personal space'* – and find those who invade it to be pushy or invasive. If we sit on a sofa in the foyer of a hotel, we don't expect anyone else to come and sit next to us without invitation. In other parts of the world, no such concept of personal space exists; I sat on a hotel sofa in Prague quite recently, and was amused and a trifle surprised to find that local people actively sought the comfort of sitting close to others, even though they were strangers, in preference to occupying other, empty seats.

consumption So we are all different, all sixty million of us. But all day, every day of our lives, we come into contact with other people and engage in some form of consumer behaviour, even if it's simply choosing between tea, coffee or a stiff drink. Once *consumption*, or even the very thought of consumption, enters the arena of our behaviour and interaction with others, we are engaging in some form of consumer behaviour. Whether reading an advertisement in a journal, watching a holiday programme on TV, eating a chocolate bar, using a mouthwash or picking out clothes from the wardrobe, we are engaging in some form of consumer behaviour. The problem is that we do so seamlessly, with no outward show of selection or choice, with the whole process that supports decision making taking place somewhere deep in our brain and utilising a series of tests and selection criteria that we may not even be aware of ourselves. Taking a step back to examine what happens in our minds, and why, has important implications for our business and social success.

Understanding how consumers think is an essential part of any proactive business, and discounting the needs and desires of our client base is a sure-fire recipe for problems. As an example, just look at the British motorcycle industry in the 1960s. The industry had prospered up to the point when British consumers made it clear that they no longer wanted the bigger, heavier, uninspiring machines that the UK was manufacturing but, instead, preferred to buy lighter, faster-revving, more economical and more reliable machines from Japan. It took years for UK manufacturers to accept that consumers were rejecting their output and, as a consequence, they handed the market on a plate to the Japanese. Today, the UK motorcycle manufacturing industry has been brought back from the brink to occupy little more than a niche market and the Japanese still largely dominate the global market.

Almost half a century later, the US car industry has ground to a halt because of mismanagement of the financial industry. The recession shouldn't have happened but, since it did, US car manufacturers are having to face the fact that they have been making cars that no one, not even the American consumer, really wants. These same consumers have been telling the motor behemoths for years that they really want what European and Far Eastern manufacturers have been selling. Will the US industry be able to restructure itself in time to survive? Time alone will tell, but it is clear that the 250 million US citizens either want, or will be forced by ecological pressures, to buy something different!

As suppliers of specialist skills and services, veterinarians are in the same position as manufacturers: if we don't supply what our consumers want, they won't buy from us. It is true that in the past clients have been *bonded* to veterinary practices, but the world has changed dramatically   *bonded* in the last fifty years, with change accelerating even more dramatically in the last decade.

Once upon a time, a percentage of cat and dog owners would come in to the practice, almost religiously, every year for a booster vaccination and a check-up for their pet. In the days before management accounting, when a practice knew how successful it was by the amount of cash in the till, the only marketing that a practice needed to do was to send out booster reminders – but those days have gone. Since the acceptance of a wider vaccination interval, clients have questioned how often they need to attend the practice, and it becomes harder for people to feel *loyalty* to any business   *loyalty* if they only use it once every two or three years. We live in a market economy which depends upon the steady *consumption* of what is offered to the masses, by the masses. For business to survive, we   *consumption* need mass consumption of products and services, but the real problem is that those masses comprise millions of *individuals*, all seeking to be recognised and treated as an *individual* in every aspect of   *individual* consumer behaviour.

Today, the principal challenge for veterinary practice is to find its own place in the broader community, to be supported by sufficient consumers to make the mathematics work and to avoid being considered as a *commodity*. If the services offered by all the practices in the UK come to be   *commodity* considered as a commodity, something that can be bought anywhere, the only differentiating factors will be price and convenience. Having some understanding of consumer behaviour is a prerequisite for ameliorating this situation but of course, if consumers want, for instance, mega-vet practices in out-of-town locations, that's what the market will provide. Consumer power has whittled away the age-old respect for all the professions and, one by one, the professions have come to accept that their role in society has been changed for them, usually without their agreement or approval.

Few of us doubt that there are profound changes in store for the veterinary profession over the next few decades. This book seeks to provide an understanding of consumers' beliefs and attitudes, why they use or purchase certain brands or services and how they choose where to buy them. This is such an essential part of marketing that to ignore these factors will inevitably lead to a misalignment with the market and eventual commercial difficulties. Most treatises on this subject are based on US experience, so in the following pages I have tried to offer a European view of the subject.

CHAPTER II
The changing world in which we (consumers) live

The changing world in which we (consumers) live

So I turned myself to face me
But I've never caught a glimpse
Of how the others must see the faker
I'm much too fast to take that test
Just gonna have to be a different man
Time may change me
But I can't trace time

David Bowie

advertising

Many years ago, I interviewed a large number of doctors, seeking their views on and their responses to a number of advertisements appearing in the medical press. Rather disconcertingly, pretty much all of them agreed that they had no views or responses, because they were professionals and were not swayed by *advertising*. Of course, many things have happened since then and I like to think that, were I to repeat the same exercise now, most if not all of them would have come to accept that every one of us is a consumer and we are all swayed, to some extent, by advertising. Even if, as a professional, one were to take the stance that it would be inappropriate to react to such advertising, I contest that it would be impossible not to experience some intellectual response.

The picture would, or wouldn't, appeal simply on the grounds of our subconscious need to gather data to inform our response.

The copy, if one read it, would or wouldn't appear well written, familiar or unfamiliar, appealing or unappealing.

conscious,
unconscious

'buying' decisions

Some response would be inevitable, whether *conscious* or *unconscious*, and that's the whole consumer argument wrapped up in a simple sentence: whether we like it or not, and whether we are aware of it or not, we are all consumers, acting in a normal, consumerist fashion. As consumers, we are making hundreds of *'buying' decisions* every hour; each time we open a magazine, look into a shop window, turn on the TV or open our wardrobes. We shouldn't confuse buying with the process of money changing hands – that's a commercial reality of some aspects of this behaviour – but every time we look at a magazine or open our wardrobe we are making a series of decisions about whether to turn the page now or look for more information, or simply which clothes to wear today. A 'buying' decision can equally effectively relate to using things we already have, to planning and holding in reserve information to be used at a later date when choosing or purchasing products or services, to taking the plunge and purchasing something from a seller now, or even to choosing which person to talk to in the bus queue. The same set of synaptic stimuli will be engaged in any of these processes, although the interpretation and/or storage of the information can differ profoundly.

perception

What has changed in the intervening years to make customers think and behave differently from the days when Alf Wight wrote *All Creatures Great and Small?* Actually, there has been a huge amount of change, some of it due to reality and some of it due to *perception*, but rather a lot of it due to a freeing-up of every individual's ability to spend money. The past twenty years have seen an explosion in personal credit, stoking the fires of economic independence that were lit after the end of World War II. When the war had ended and the dust settled, people in the UK found that much of the class system that had previously applied had been swept away, leaving widespread support for egalitarianism. Most importantly, every family and individual had shared in the horrors of the war and in the camaraderie and sharing that had affected everyone from fighting men and women to those left picking up the pieces at home. The net result was a nation of individuals who felt that they could succeed with hard work and application and without the rigid class divides that had compartmentalised people according to their education, background and genetics. For the first time, people sensed the optimism that came from opportunity, and with it came a need to regenerate employment to restore the fabric of the country. Increased employment and opportunity created

acquisition more wealth and higher spending. Higher spending created awareness among a populace eager to be recognised for its new standing, and this fuelled a desire to acquire the same things as friends and neighbours had. Avarice is hardly a newly invented sin and, post-war, the end of a period of abstinence from spending and *acquisition*, together with new opportunities and higher awareness, created an explosion of desire to enjoy a wide range of products and services that had hitherto been unavailable or, perhaps, only available to a select few.

Suddenly, anything was possible, although the real explosion in consumption didn't happen until people put away their traditional insistence on saving for spending rather than borrowing the money to facilitate the purchase. Phrases like 'on the never-never' and 'having it on tick' were new to the UK, whereas the idea of Christmas Club saving can be traced much further back than the 1950s. This explosion in people's willingness to borrow money to bring forward a purchase stemmed from the widespread need to borrow money to buy new homes after the war and also from a gradual diminution of the influence of the Church in people's lives. Where the Church had been most present, the scriptures, with their admonitions against profligacy and avarice, had maintained the strongest influence over people's attitudes, but as that influence began to wane, so there was less and less opposition in society to the appeal of instant gratification, and the idea of unfettered consumption spread like wildfire.

When I was a child, our house didn't have a television, but I went, with all the other children in the street, to a neighbour's house to watch the Coronation of Queen Elizabeth II on their new television. This was in February 1952, and by the end of that year almost every house in the street owned a television. Roughly the same timespan occurred between the first of our social contacts acquiring a car, a washing machine and a radiogram on which to play the vinyl 78 rpm records that people suddenly discovered, and everyone we knew having some example or another of the same thing. Not only did we all want a television, a car or a washing machine, we all wanted a better one than the people next door, in a form of spending one-upmanship.

Of course, we were not without a great deal of assistance in developing our new-found love affair with acquisition. In the 1960s, the humble trading stamp burst onto the scene in the form of Green Shield stamps. These were offered free of charge by retailers to add value to their market offering and to encourage loyalty from their client base. It was a great way for retailers to differentiate themselves. and suddenly individuals felt that they had increased importance to the retailer and that they were themselves people of means whose business was being actively courted. The craze for collecting these stamps and claiming free gifts from a catalogue of items spread like wildfire, as our avarice and lust for various items grew and the pound in our pockets took on a higher value (though only in our heads, as one needed hundreds of completed books of stamps to be able to exchange them for something quite small but nonetheless free). I remember, as a young person, feeling that there was something slightly forbidden about all this – but that simply fuelled the fires of desire!

For big items of expenditure we rapidly became familiar with the idea of hire purchase, but for smaller everyday acquisitions we had to look no further than the USA, where the credit card had been created during the 1930s and had become well established by the 1950s. Because the UK bought movies and television programmes from the US, it was plain for all to see that everyone in the USA lived like kings, with luxurious houses, huge cars and every labour-saving device known to man. It wasn't long before everyone in the UK wanted the same things, and with the advent of independent commercial television in 1955 we soon became used to seeing regular advertisements for things we didn't know we wanted. There were fourteen regional franchises distributing ITV from Penzance to Penicuik, and our conversion to an acquisitive society happened almost overnight. By the end of the 1960s, we had the desire to acquire things long before we could afford to buy them, encouragement from advertisers and retailers that it was normal to feel this way, and the wherewithal thanks to hire purchase, overdrafts and credit cards to do so.

As savings declined and spending increased, people found it easier and easier to justify their spending both to themselves and to others, and in this process an essential part of consumer behaviour was born. The concept, to quote a hair products advertisement, 'because you're worth it' is a fundamental part of the consumer process. No one can successfully spend money on themselves if they believe that they are unworthy recipients of the goods or services purchased. Instead, we seek solace and satisfaction from the act of purchasing, which acts rather like an artificial endorphin: just as our massive national consumption of chocolate revolves around the notion of self-reward, so the act of buying something, if all the component parts come together into a successful experience, is both satisfying and rewarding. The phrase '*retail therapy*' reflects this concept admirably.   '*retail therapy*'

It is clear that the principal influences on the development of this process of self-reward have been many and complex. If we look back at the UK in the 1950s, family structure was paramount; the influence of both the State and the Church was not just stronger but inherent in a code of behaviour that was unwritten but universally recognised. Sixty years ago, social categorisation was normal and for many people their horizon was to some extent established by the social group into which they had been born. Today, in contrast, the mantra of every concerned parent is to drum into their offspring the realisation that if they want anything badly enough, they can achieve it. Some of us remember Prince Charles expostulating against the unrealistic nature of this idea in the late 1990s, stressing that innate talent, willingness and an ability to learn, together with access to the means of achieving such greatness, are all factors which cannot be dismissed. Nevertheless, it is the case that British folklore now holds as an established fact that, in the UK, anyone is free to achieve greatness, in any field, if they work hard enough. Of course, this is not a purely British phenomenon and is in fact something which Britons have picked up from watching the American TV programmes purchased to fill the programming hours of British TV channels.

In the USA, of course, the idea that anyone can make good is a fundamental tenet of a constitution that was set up to encourage huge numbers of migrant workers to achieve, in their new land, whatever had been denied them in their countries of birth. This is a fundamental part of every American's psyche, introduced to them in the cradle and measured and assessed throughout their lives. What seemed normal on American TV seemed strange and intoxicating for a nation of Britons whose *social memory*, i.e. that behaviour and thinking which society appears to accept and require,   *social memory* was still imbued with pre-war Britain, where the country's rulers were nearly all from a privileged background and where socialism, however attractive to those who had few assets, was still frowned upon and discouraged by those who controlled society.

Here, then, was a mechanism, brought willingly and without question into our homes, that complicated the normal way of thinking. I recall that my grandmother disapproved of commercial TV and would only let us watch BBC programmes, as she considered TV paid for by advertising to be socially reprehensible. It's impossible to think in these terms today, but such thinking was remarkably widespread in the late 1950s.

With American TV programming came glorious glimpses of another world where people all lived in huge houses, owned shiny new cars and, best of all for British women, had a whole raft of labour-saving devices such as washing machines and vacuum cleaners. What nation wouldn't sink into a quiet frenzy of avarice? Why wouldn't every Briton want what his or her American cousins simply took for granted? As the population grew and employment became more assured, credit became more readily available and people's perceptions of what might be became more focused on what actually was possible. The nation was getting to its feet after the privations of wartime and people wanted a return to the brief period of camaraderie and equality that had characterised some aspects of behaviour during the Second World War. The weary celebrations of victory had given way to the reality that both the UK and its people needed to build a new future, and very few people wanted to go back to a class-ridden society conducted by the many for the benefit of the few. Pandora's box had been well and truly opened by the 1950s and, once released, there was nothing that could be done to get the fates back into the box.

There was a massive awareness that things had to be rebuilt, a widespread willingness to work hard to achieve something, a weakening of the bonds of both Church and State, and the beginnings of a real liberation for women, who both could and chose to go out to work – a means of setting aside the old order. Add to this the sweetshop nature of TV programmes imported from the wealthy and aspirational USA and a new life form began to emerge. If women were to go to work, surely some assistance in the form of labour-saving devices was a perfectly rational aspiration, and if our new enthusiasm for work as a means of rebuilding society and advancing the cause of our own families and selves was to become a paramount commitment, individuals sought to differentiate themselves by variations in the clothing they wore, the cars that they were now able to own, the make-up or perfume they used, the houses they lived in, the way they could furnish and decorate them, the gardens they had, the holidays they could take and the new types of food they could buy – the list was endless. Every sector involved in this list could be developed into a new industry, and the more people earned, the more they bought, fuelling the redevelopment of not just the UK but also its trading partners.

For the sake of convenience, let's say that this was the time when rampant consumerism was born in the UK. It was clearly embryonic compared with the levels of desire and fulfilment apparent today, but all the factors were present to create a new form of social behaviour. In mainland Europe, progress was different for a whole raft of reasons, and people there demonstrated some resistance

to adopting these innovations.[1] Invasion by a foreign power had not only destroyed much of the fabric of their countries but had also robbed them of many of the social and cultural keys to their civilisation, resulting in an interim period of some decades while these nations re-established the building blocks of their national identities. The power of both State and Church was stronger in many countries, and economic rebuilding was slower in some places, although the Marshall Plan enabled Germany to rebuild quickly and more completely. This gave Germany a massive economic advantage within the emergent Europe of these post-war years and made German social and individual prosperity a form of role model for Europe, in much the same way as Britons looked to the US for consumerist stimuli. As a result, Britain has always been far more American in its approach, aided no doubt by a common language, and twenty years ago it would have been said that, in social trends, the US would lead, followed by Britain ten years later and with the rest of Europe following on after a further decade.

brands

More recently, a kind of invisible divide has taken place, with Northern Europe closing the gap rapidly on the UK, Southern European countries still a little behind and more galvanised by issues reflecting their national identity, and Central and Eastern Europe bringing up the rear. Of course, nothing is straightforward and many factors affect this explosion in consumerism and the way it is unfolding across an enlarged Europe. Visit any major city anywhere in Europe and the big *brands* are all evident: Louis Vuitton, Ferrari, Sheraton, Four Seasons, Bollinger, Chanel and Prada are all alive and well in Milan, Madrid, Munich and Moscow just as they are in Manchester.

affluence

Where people have money, they seek to display their own personalised *affluence* to differentiate themselves, and others who have less still seek to catch up and to be seen to be doing so. In Southern Europe, however, the power of the Catholic Church remains stronger, and throughout Europe the spread of Islam has had a significant effect. In some countries, secularisation remains difficult, even though there are mounting pressures to reduce religious influence on social life. Some of these pressures come from outside the country and are universal, given the instantaneous nature of TV pictures and the Internet. Others come from inside the country, as a new Islamic middle class has been created through the increasing success of the national economy. With the accumulation of wealth and assets, this emergent group, while conservative in its values, is far less conservative in its consumption.

Islam's

What is new here, and previously unrecognised by Western consumer society, is *Islam's* application of a consumerist approach as it reaches out into the twenty-first century. Fashion is a good example of how a new segment can be created almost overnight. Islamic tradition, based on the Koran, had defined what form of dress would be acceptable, and this remained unchallenged for hundreds of years. Today's generation seeks to find different interpretations of the recommended practices and to find an acceptable diversity in dress through these different interpretations. As in any society, diversity of dress enables the adherents of each different style to classify themselves as belonging to a like-minded group, and, as these different interpretations become more widely recognised and accepted, new styles of dress allow people to demonstrate their religious adherence and individuality at the same time as meeting the needs of rapidly emerging economic success.

Islamic women can differentiate themselves from Western women, as is required of them, and, additionally, can create a mechanism through fashion for distancing themselves from what they may perceive as cultural backwardness. Turkey is a good example of how, by straddling the demands of both Islam and the wider European horizon, women have developed a fashion industry of their own, as part of an expansive embracing of consumerism on their own terms.[2]

REFERENCES

1 W.D. Hoyer and D.J. MacInnis, *Consumer behavior*, 2nd edition; Houghton Mifflin, 2001

2 E. Arnould, L. Price and G. Zinkhan, *Consumers,* 2nd edition; McGraw-Hill, 2004

CHAPTER III
What is the market?

What is the market?

Money, money, money
Always sunny
In the rich man's world
Aha-ahaaa
All the things I could do
If I had a little money
It's a rich man's world

Abba

That almost sounds like a silly question: surely we're all familiar with the idea of a *market*? In fact, the concept of trading, buying and selling to supply our needs or desires, is as old as the hills. When men graduated from nipping out of their cave and bashing a passing mammal on the head to provide food for the family, they took a pivotal step in the maturing of early human society. In a hunter-gatherer culture the primary method of subsistence involves the direct sourcing of edible plants and animals from the wild, foraging and hunting without significant recourse to the domestication of either. Hunter-gatherers obtain more from gathering than from hunting: up to 80% of their food is obtained by gathering,[1] and in primitive times such food could not easily be stored or moved from one place to another, which in turn fostered the development of small, local communities clustered around the supply of food.

What historians call the Neolithic Revolution – the transition from hunter-gatherer communities and bands to agriculture and settlement – constituted the first agricultural revolution, with the earliest developments probably taking place in the Middle East around 10,000 BC. The most interesting innovation was the concept of surplus supply. Wouldn't people's development of different skills and varying abilities to generate supplies of various foodstuffs naturally lead to an early type of market, where they could barter their supplies or skills for some reciprocal benefit? In its earliest form, it would have been sufficient for the market to amass quantities of similar produce for exchange, and the likelihood is that the produce would have been far from uniform in size and quality, with little or no differentiation between suppliers other than whatever relationship might have been established.

If no differentiation is possible or even desirable in a marketplace, the goods or services on offer become simple commodities, with *price* and *convenience* being the principal drivers for business. If all we want is an empty cardboard box, none of us is going to drive twenty kilometres to buy one from a trader if one can be found fifty metres away. If, however, having handles on the box is a really important feature for you, you may be prepared to sacrifice convenience and, to some extent, price to

get the one you want. This is *market segmentation* at its simplest, and from very early in the development of barter as a means of trade some people will have developed a liking for redder apples, browner eggs or creamier milk; thus, together with segmentation, the embryonic concept of

consumer choice and selection will have arisen in the early marketplace.

How does the marketplace operate? Michael Solomon writes about *role theory*,[2] which puts forward the view that much of consumer behaviour resembles actions in a play, whereby each consumer has the lines, scenes, costumes and props necessary to put on a good performance. People often play more than one role in making the decision to purchase, acquire or adopt something, and thus they may amend the decision process to reflect the particular play that they are performing in at that moment. This can be something as fundamental as feeling the need to act in a certain way, different from the way you were acting before the moment when someone you know joined in the decision process. Of course, the decision criteria are not fixed; they may be significantly adaptable and, therefore, differ according to the roles people are playing.

So, going back to our Neolithic marketplace, if someone were to exhibit a preference for redder

'buyer behaviour'
apples, this would have been an early manifestation of *'buyer behaviour'*, representing some form of interaction between the buyer and seller, notwithstanding the currency of barter or cash. If such an

exchange
interaction were repeated, the process would have developed into an *'exchange'*, in which a number of people choose to operate the interaction to recognise something which has perceived value within the marketplace. This is a fundamental concept of marketing which, in turn, revolves around the availability of 'consumers' to drive the process by identifying their needs and desires in order for someone else to satisfy them. Of course, today's consumers have a vast array of choices which far exceeds the dreams of our Neolithic counterparts, and with that comes significant refinement in the way consumers make their purchasing decisions.

Not every consumer will act as an individual all the time, although every consumer is an individual at all times. Confusing? Imagine that the board of a company has decided to purchase a new computer server to host its website. The board will refine and define its purchasing criteria, provide budget guidance and set a timeline for acquisition. It may then instruct the IT manager to make the purchase, and the manager will in turn approach four mainstream suppliers. The basics of the deal are already done, with the IT manager having little room for financial manoeuvre, but in the end the deal may be struck with the least competitive of the four simply for reasons of convenience, such as the sales executive or technical manager living nearby and thus being better able to service the account. A number of people will have had some input into that purchasing decision, but in the end it can simply come down to a relationship – either long-standing or nascent – making the decision happen. With the advent of the Internet, not only are our needs and desires shaped by outside forces, but they might now be met by marketers from around the globe. With choice comes complication, and some people will choose to reduce the complication by adding their own personal filter to this process, for examples by opting to 'Buy British' or to buy only from local suppliers.

Is this enough background to attempt a definition of consumer behaviour? It has been defined as 'the study of the processes involved when individuals or groups select, purchase, use or dispose of products, services, ideas or experiences to satisfy needs or desires'.[3] Consumer behaviour seems as widely variable as there are consumers to operate it, so why bother with trying to understand it? In its simplest form, the answer must be that understanding consumer behaviour is good for business. If we accept that individuals and groups of consumers have needs and that business revolves around providing some way of satisfying these needs, it is surely necessary to understand and anticipate the needs and desires of the people or businesses one is planning to sell to. The alternative is to operate a business on the premise that consumers are quite frankly lucky to be able to come here at all. Does that sound inflexible, archaic and way out of touch with reality? Of course it does, yet how many veterinary practices seem to operate along these lines, with ancillary staff apparently trained or tolerated in the practice of keeping clients at bay 'because we're busy'?

In the process of refining his or her purchasing decisions, every consumer wants and expects to be treated as an individual. We all recognise that it is necessary somehow to segment the vast available market of billions of potential customers into more convenient market segments in which consumers share similar preferences, but it is equally important to see this segmentation of the market as merely convenient, faintly drawn pencil lines which provide some means of separating groups of preferences and then to revert to treating consumers as individuals within these groupings. Because we absolutely do not want the veterinary market to become a trading ground for commodities, it is imperative that practitioners refine their market offering to meet the identified needs of identifiable groups of individual consumers, all of whom have similar needs and expectations, and that they seek to establish brand loyalty in the process. Consumer uptake is the acid test of any marketing strategy, and so understanding one's consumers is a prerequisite even for formulating the strategy in the first place, let alone defining one's business parameters to adhere to the strategy.

If we are to encourage brand loyalty, first we need a clearly defined 'brand'. Every veterinary practice trading in the marketplace is in itself a brand. It has recognisable qualities, a consumer-facing persona all of its own. While many veterinary surgeons don't feel that they need to have a reproducible brand, consumers will be looking either for something that they recognise and are familiar with, or for something that jumps off the page and appeals to them in some way. Consumers look for a 'brand personality', a set of traits or qualities which they can attribute to a product as if it were a person. 'Brand loyalty' is created when people like these traits or qualities so much that they *brand loyalty* will consciously choose to repeat the purchasing experience on more than one occasion. However, this in turn depends entirely on something called '*brand equity*', which means that the brand enjoys *brand equity* strong positive associations in a consumer's memory and will command loyalty as a result.

No one will wish to repeat a painful exercise if the alternative of a positive one, or even just the prospect of a more positive one, is available. Thus each and every one of us trading our brands in the marketplace is only as good as the last experience our consumers had with us. The world of cricket provides a good analogy: no matter how good-looking and well marketed a country's batsmen might be, their continued selection is entirely dependent upon their last innings. In the world of the consumer, everything changes with some frequency, and indeed, in some industries such as fashion or cars, the product is changed frequently in order to stimulate desire and to prompt another purchasing event. So it's necessary not just to develop an attractive and persuasive brand, but to be constantly watching for changes in consumer behaviour, so that this new knowledge can be used to adapt and refine our brand offering to meet changes in consumers' needs and desires. If this sounds daunting, it may help to remember that it isn't really new. It has been this way since mankind discovered that some people had redder apples than others; the only difference is that changes in consumer expectation are coming about faster than ever, so to maintain our own '*brand community*' *brand community* we now need a better understanding of the values of those consumers who share a set of social relationships which reflect a common interest in using our particular brand.

Whether we like it or not, we all live in a world where consumer choice is influenced by a myriad outside pressures. Just as our elders did in the immediate post-war period, today's consumers shape their desires, sometimes confusing desires with needs, by absorbing marketing stimuli from the various media that surround us all. In a household with pets, the threat of flea infestation is a constant one, particularly as our homes are so hospitable to the little visitors. Most of us would accept that we do actually need to eradicate any infestation when we see or feel its presence. The need to stop the development of flea larvae and hence reproduction of the flea is both a convincing, rational argument and a 'nice to have', but, at the point of biting either the pets or ourselves, the fleas clearly demonstrate the immediate need for the biting to stop. Marketing campaigns have, however, very successfully established the concept of regular quarterly treatment of all animals, bedding and furniture in consumers' minds. It is good for the pharmaceutical industry, good for the fortunes of veterinary practice and, in general terms, good for most pet owners. But is it actually a genuine need or merely something that is portrayed as a win:win for most parties?

From a business point of view, it probably doesn't matter, as long as pet owners buy more product. For the veterinary surgeon, there is both a scientific and a professional overlay to this process which may on occasion raise some scintilla of doubt or pricking of conscience on behalf of the client, and this is where it becomes so much more difficult for the veterinary practitioner than for the pet store, saddler, groomer or supermarket, which may be selling the same flea treatments. Without doubt, these other retail establishments will have no concerns over whether consumers buy the right amount or fifty times the correct amount of product, but it would be an unusual veterinary surgeon who felt the same way.

The overlay of such professional concerns inevitably means that the veterinary surgeon cannot able to compete on a level playing field with other retailers, which makes a nonsense of government's attempts to impose the self-regulation of market forces on the profession. However, for as long as the veterinary profession chooses to sell products as well as its other skills and services, it will need to find ways of developing a different kind of relationship with its consumers in order to facilitate the sale of products which are coming to be seen as commodities. In the days when veterinary surgeons had all the effective products and other retailers had largely ineffective ones, life was comparatively easy, but those days are rapidly disappearing. In today's world, whether we like it or not, veterinary surgeons need to understand their consumers and consumer behaviour just as much as (and probably even more than) other competitive retailers.

internet If only life were that simple and all we had to do was to keep a wary eye on what our competitors down the road were doing! Life has moved on in a big way, thanks to the *Internet*, and sadly, like most amazing inventions, the Internet has proved to be something of a two-edged sword for the veterinary practitioner. Not only can every consumer who wishes to do so approach each consultation clutching a sheaf of downloaded diagnostics to assist you in making the necessary decisions, but the Internet provides a mechanism for two other cherished consumer actions: it allows them to believe that they are sufficiently informed to command an exchange of views on an equal basis with the professional they are talking to, and it allows them to change the relationship so that they are seeking your advice with the express intention of making the decisions themselves. Thus the Internet has simultaneously informed and empowered consumers, at the same time as giving them a mechanism to check your pricing against the universe of competition.

virtual The Internet has created a *virtual* shopping mall at the click of a mouse. Not only can consumers check your pricing, they can buy from anywhere in the world products which are perceived to be, or may actually be, the same as the products you sell. Of course there are constraints on the sale of pharmaceuticals that require a prescription, but in reality not all retailers of prescription drugs are as ethical as you are. Veterinary surgeons reading these pages may well feel aggrieved at having to compete with both hands tied behind their backs, at having the ongoing costs associated with staffing a building, equipping it with expensive equipment, meeting the demands of employment law, health and safety and satisfying the requirements of being a member of the RCVS, but it's a fact that consumers neither understand nor care about that. In their perception, your entry on the Google page is no different from the hundreds of others displayed. In marketing terms this is a sterile environment, where there can be no real relationship and where there are no visual clues to help steer a discussion to a successful climax, but for consumers it is the ultimate in convenience. Here they can shop all day, every day, without getting out of bed. There are no barriers to what is possible other than the limits of what is available, and the choice is vast. Now, with Internet-enabled handheld devices, the same access is available to consumers wherever they may be, adding significantly to their convenience.

Just as we have tried, through conventional marketing, to create brand communities around our various businesses, we are now faced with virtual consumer communities to whom we have to appeal if we are also to succeed in this new marketplace. Not every practice will choose to do so, one can imagine a situation where some practices may take the decision not to attempt to compete in certain areas, particularly the sale of commodity products such as flea and worm treatments, food and other ancillary products.

marketing mix In essence, this is just a different way of compiling the *marketing mix* for your brand and, while it narrows the opportunities for sale and subsequent income, it also frees up space and employee time and provides a renewed focus for the development of professional services and their marketing to brand communities seeking these services.

If, however, the practice does choose to compete in these areas, it would pay the principals to take a close look at the tools and methods used by other online competitors in different market *rewards* sectors. Amazon, for instance, *rewards* regular traders with ratings to demonstrate their reliability, while other sites, such as Hardens, bond users to the business by inviting their own reviews of establishments; thus their restaurant review publications come to represent the critical acclaim not just of professional inspectors but also of the very people who regularly and routinely use the products. In this world, e-consumers have enormous power. They have no constraints of geography, time or place. They have ready and immediate access to countless thousands of similarly minded people who, with the same e-communication skills, can help them to access literally millions more people. With the advent of the blog, anyone can be a journalist, a restaurant reviewer or, without too much exaggeration, trial judge, jury and PR agency all rolled into one.

There has never been a time in the history of mankind when there was greater opportunity to market one's own brand in so many ways or to such an enormous audience. We simply have to take

the time to get our mind around what we want to achieve and then to utilise the appropriate tools and skills to achieve it.

REFERENCES

1 R.B. Lee, I. DeVore and J. Nash-Mitchell, *Man the Hunter*; Wenner Grenn Foundation for Anthropological Research, Aldine, 1968
2 M.R. Solomon, 'The role of products as social stimuli; a symbolic interactionism perspective', in *Journal of Consumer Research* 10, 1983
3 M.R. Solomon, *Consumer behaviour – buying, having and being*, 8th edition; Pearson Education, 2009

CHAPTER IV
Consumers in the veterinary arena

Consumers in the veterinary arena

If they don't give me proper credit
I just walk away

They can beg and they can plead
But they can't see the light, that's right
'Cause the boy with the cold hard cash
Is always Mister right'

Madonna

PATTERNS, TRENDS AND CHANGES IN BEHAVIOUR

I wonder how many parents sit at their breakfast table and shake their heads in amazement, or bemusement, at the conversation or behaviour of their teenage offspring and their friends. It's a trifle unfair, because age and the passing of time have dulled our own recollection of how we were and what we said when we were teenagers ourselves, but one thing is clear: things are different now! Teenagers make a great subject for social study, as they exemplify much that is extreme and, by and large, do so in fairly predictable ways. Some clear patterns emerge from very little observation, and as parents we all find out, sooner or later, that other parents usually see a far better side of our offspring's behaviour than we do. Clearly, most teenagers behave in a more difficult fashion when they're at home, largely because they can. Away from the constraints of school, college, work or the presence of other adults, many teenagers feel they can behave with more abandon at home, largely because they know that their parents are more likely to indulge them and allow them to get away with more aberrant behaviour. With other children's parents they are almost always extremely polite and well behaved. Frustrating, isn't it?

codes of behaviour

Similar, though usually less extreme patterns can be found in consumer behaviour, where different *codes of behaviour* are adopted by many different groups. Young children can be very powerful influencers of their parents' behaviour – how many times have we all seen, or experienced, a small child performing an elaborate and well practised pantomime to get sweets in a supermarket? Some will create mayhem all the way around the aisles, simply to ensure that they receive sweets at the checkout from a harassed parent. Others will behave impeccably until the parent is preoccupied with transferring goods from the trolley to the checkout and will then start a repetitive litany of demands, building in volume and petulance until the parent gives in. Like pets, they do it because it works almost every time.

In the post office, I am amazed how often older people will queue jump and will look at you as if to dare you to challenge them. Perhaps, having lived through lengthy periods of war and deprivation, some of them think they deserve special attention – and who could blame them? But the same logic probably applies: perhaps they behave in this way because they can!

People from different cultures also behave differently. In Germany, awareness of the ecological impact of packaging and the cost of disposing of it encourages many people to select products with minimal external packaging and, in some cases, to strip off decorative, non-functional packaging and leave it in the shop for that business to dispose of. In parts of Britain with a large Asian population, women shopping for clothes will often be seen taking folded garments out of their wrappers and opening them up to feel the quality. French consumers wouldn't dream of buying peaches without feeling them first, but this wreaks havoc with the rigid plastic packaging used by some British supermarkets at the point of sale to protect the fruit from bruising.

In New York, if a meal is not considered up to standard, diners will let their views be heard quite volubly, yet in Britain, should something not meet our expectation, we are usually content to vote with our feet and vow, silently of course, never to return. What is more, it is not uncommon for

people in the UK, when asked if everything is all right with a meal, to deny any problems, say that things are fine when they clearly are not, and then vote with their feet. The confrontation that is both expected and widely accepted in one culture is considered taboo in another.

Clearly, there is no right or wrong about any of this; each society is just a microcosm in which people follow the local rules which are considered acceptable. However, things are changing rapidly, and actions which would once have been considered unacceptable are now the norm in our polyglot, fast-moving society. In a smart London veterinary practice, one principal complained to me that not only could he not get veterinary surgeons to work the extended hours needed to meet the demands of his ever less tolerant client base, but additionally the slightest delay or lateness would be greeted by clients with an open display of impatience, sighing, dramatic consultation of watches and tapping of fingers and feet. The fact that this is in an upmarket, fiendishly expensive part of North London may be relevant, because people with more money tend to expect to be treated better – but better than whom, I wonder? Better than the other people sitting there, all of whom are similarly well off? *urban consumers* It has become a noticeable trait of *urban consumers* that they consider their time to be very precious *rural* and expect a more snappy, timely service than their *rural* counterparts, who seem far more comfortable with, and understanding of, delay and a generally slower pace.

I moved quite recently from a London suburb to Worcestershire, where, for three months of the year, the whole outdoors seemed to smell of onions or manure and the biggest, most obvious change was the speed at which people drive. Here, people seem to drive at exactly 10 mph below the legal limit for the road they are on, with the exception of motorways, where they adhere to the 70 mph limit as if it were part of their religion. There's nothing wrong with that, but it's a huge contrast from what I had been used to in the urban environment, where everyone drives as if they were a racing driver, consideration for others is for pussies and the most common hand signal would, if obeyed, bring about a burgeoning population.

Experiments with rats and pigs show that if you confine large numbers of either species to a small space, they become irritable and argumentative. Humans behave similarly, but we often forget *environment* that people's behaviour is affected by their *environment*. Very busy roads make for no-time-for– breakfast mornings, unpredictable delays, lateness for work or other activities, high blood pressure and general irritability, so why are we surprised when this is what happens? The rural idyll often makes for an early-to-bed, early-rising, cooked-breakfast way of life which leaves people blissfully unaware of whatever was on TV after News at Ten, even if it has got the nation in a twitter. Now, while all that applies to ourselves, it also applies just as much to Mrs Smith, and to her cat at the other end of the scale.

Veterinary surgeons often complain that Mrs Smith didn't seem to be taking in what they were telling her and that, judging by the lack of compliance since the last consultation, very little *communication* information seemed to survive the journey back home. If *communication* is a problem, we shouldn't simply assume that Mrs Jones is a slice short of a full loaf. Perhaps part of the problem is that Mrs Jones, sitting in the waiting room with her cat, wasn't gearing up for a session on Mastermind, specialist subject tubules and nephrons. Instead, she was probably wondering what to cook for the children's tea, what was likely to happen about their dispute with the neighbour who throws cat faeces back over the fence, and whether she had turned off the gas that morning. Consumers have refined their behaviour over the last fifty years or so: they now store and process huge quantities of information, but deal with each and every item of data in a transient manner, lacking much depth or application.

This is just one of the reasons why adults find it so difficult to return to any serious studies after leaving school, or even to read an intellectually demanding book. It is also the reason why, as is well recognised in the medical field, patients consulting their GP forget more than 40% of what they have been told by the doctor before they close the consulting room door and anything up to 80% by the time they get home. Medics solve this problem by displaying a vast number of leaflets explaining various diseases and conditions and making sure that patients take some written material home with them as an aide-memoire. Of course, there's also the issue of communication skills and how well the veterinary profession has been trained in these vital skills, but that's another topic altogether.

Much consumer behaviour depends on what is considered acceptable conduct in society as a whole, embracing the cultural norms of everyday life and influences from TV, film, online sources and other stimuli. If you asked most middle-aged people ten years ago how often they would buy something via the Internet, very few people would have said anything other than 'never', yet now the Internet accounts for a huge percentage of sales and the group known as 'silver surfers' (pensioners) is among the highest users of the Internet, if not necessarily of online purchasers.

Why do people buy on the Internet? What happened to change behaviour so much and so quickly? One of the first studies of Internet purchasing was conducted in 1999 in the USA, where Internet usage was already much higher than in the UK. The first Wharton Virtual Test Market survey panel (WVTM1) was closely matched to the US online population.[1] Responses from 9,738 panellists provided a basis for identifying factors that predicted whether a person bought goods or services online and, if so, how much they spent. Based on logic and regression analysis of the data, two major categories of variables emerged as predictors of online buying and spending: '*time starvation*' and a '*wired*' lifestyle.[2]

The researchers found that *online buyers* worked many hours each week (e.g. a single person working over 50 hours per week or a married couple working over 100 hours per week). Because such 'time-starved' panellists had fewer hours available for leisure, the study concluded that they made purchases on the Internet to save time. People who bought online also used the Internet more widely than other Internet users: they led a more 'wired' lifestyle. They used email to keep in touch with family and friends. They had been on the Internet for years. compared to months for non-buyers. And, finally, they used the Internet regularly at work and believed it had improved their productivity. The study also found that the percentage of panellists making a purchase on the Internet increased as a function of time spent online. The greater the amount of time spent online, the greater the chance of making a purchase online.

Bearing in mind that this research was published a decade ago, the results were a surprising

time starvation
'wired' lifestyle
online buyers

harbinger of what we have since come to recognise as normal consumer behaviour. As an example, more than 75% of all new car purchases are made after previous consultation of the Internet, leading to a fascinating change in retail patterns whereby people seek out information about certain models on websites such as www.edmunds.com, then go to hugely expensive showrooms to see and test drive the cars, and subsequently revert to the Internet to source the best financial deals.

Nowadays, not only do many (or even most?) of us buy our airline tickets on line, book hotels on line, find out about travel, train timetables and routes, motorway delays and school snow closures *social networking* on line, but the staggering popularity of multifarious *social networking* sites has overwhelmed traditional advertising, bringing chaos and uncertainty to conventional commercial TV companies. Whether they use Facebook, Twitter or any of the host of social networking media, millions of people are willing and keen to build online profiles of themselves, giving sometimes intimate details of their lives and activities for unknown millions to click on. In rather the same way as we behave differently in the 'safe' cocoon of our motor cars, acting in a far more confrontational and aggressive manner because we feel ourselves to be untouchable, millions of people disclose highly personal information for the world to see, in a way that they would simply not do if meeting an unknown person face to face. We live in an age in which minor celebrity is celebrated and countless people enhance their sense of self-worth by writing personal blogs on line, by uploading photographs of themselves and their friends and by posting descriptions of their social lives, where they've been, who they've met and other triumphs on the social scene. In these ways, people's perceptions of their standing and self-worth subtly change, and this in turn affects they way they interact with one another in formal and less formal circumstances.

How people treat other, faceless, nameless people across the ether has an inevitable effect on how they interact when they are face to face. Just as written correspondence has an abbreviated style which is acceptable on the Internet and is becoming more acceptable in everyday life, so online interactive behaviour is coming to form a bigger and bigger part of people's behaviour in normal life too. When today's students go off to university, they will have met and made friends with the people they will be sharing accommodation with long before they ever arrive at the hall of residence. Young people now conduct lengthy courtships by text and on Facebook before they go on to progress the *online security* relationship face to face. The extent of *online security*, for the protection of both data and vulnerable people, is testament to the power and reach of the Internet into our lives and its effect on 'normal' behaviour.

Clearly, there are a myriad influences on consumer behaviour. Whether they come from other races *multicultural society* and cultures in our increasingly *multicultural society*, from aspects of age-related behaviour whereby pensioners seek eternal youth and youths seek other ways to differentiate themselves, or from geographical factors such as urban versus rural demographics; whether they arise from a shift in values from a professional-led society to one that celebrates cash regardless of its origins, or from the relaxation of social norms relating to sex, drugs, alcohol and public behaviour; whether they derive from foreign (largely US-led) urban trends in clothing, music, language and behaviour, or

from new behavioural norms gleaned from TV, film and the Internet; whatever their source, these influences stir a pot which is constantly evolving.

Why do these patterns and trends matter to the veterinary practitioner? Of course, in one sense, they don't matter much at all. If, as a practitioner, all you want to do is open your doors and treat whatever comes through them as and when, the world can continue to spin with as many changes taking place as there are minutes in the day. If, on the other hand, you want to plan your business, take the view that you wish to retain clients, attract more new ones that you lose and operate your veterinary practice as a competitive and progressive business, you have no choice but to attempt to understand these changes in behaviour and ride this wave of change, adapting your offering to meet new demands and new standards of service and convenience.

CONSUMER ACTIVITY IN EVERYDAY LIFE

If you are fortunate or unfortunate enough, depending on your viewpoint, to live within twenty miles of a major city, the chances are that someone in your family commutes to work in that city. Although suburbia is well served by road and rail transport, journey times inevitably get longer and longer as more factors come into play: density of traffic, peak flow times, restrictions and problems with road or track are just some of the difficulties that commuters have to deal with on a daily basis. On top of all this, the UK has increasingly adopted an American style of business in which existing staff often have to fill the gap when someone leaves without being replaced or when others are made redundant. The result is that Britain works longer hours than most other European countries, which have signed up to the EU's Social Chapter (see table 4.1).[3] This is without taking into consideration the need for overtime, which is particularly important to the large number of employees on lower wages.

Table 4.1: Average working hours per week

Average working hours per week							
UK	43.6	Greece	40.8	Spain	40.6	Portugal	40.6
Austria	40.2	Sweden	40.1	Germany	40.1	Ireland	40
Luxembourg	39.7	France	39.6	Finland	39.3	Netherlands	39
Denmark	38.9	Italy	38.5	Belgium	38.4		

Source: Workplace Employee Relations Survey 1998

The end result is that, for many of us, getting to the vet with our animals is simply not possible during the week, unless the vet stays open till 8 pm or later. In certain parts of the country there would be little point in opening the practice doors between 10 am and 5 pm unless we needed the custom of pensioners, the unemployed and those with children at school. In other parts of the country, and in practices situated in or near large housing estates where there are many families with small children, the workload is driven by puppies and kittens and there is little practice traffic after 6 pm. We shouldn't leap to conclusions, however: while business in the commuter belt is loaded towards unsocial hours, these consumers often fall into one of two conveniently labelled categories:

- cash rich and time poor
- time rich and cash poor

Consumers in the former category are ready and willing to pay for service and convenience, and in the USA the provision of mobile veterinary surgeries calling on clients at a time to suit their lifestyles can be big business. Those in the latter category, which probably encompasses young parents, pensioners and the unemployed together with those working from home, levels of service and convenience are less important than other aspects of the business relationship.

Twenty years ago, most practices set their charges as a formulaic reaction to those of their nearest competitors and the declared hours of business were largely the same across the board. Now, however, practitioners need to understand their businesses far better: it's vital to know what costs are being incurred and to pitch charges at a level that gives an adequate margin over costs, to ensure that a profit is actually generated. Whether consumers will, in turn, accept these costs and bring their business to the higher-charging practices is a critical factor in the success of numerous practices across the country. It is very common for vets to examine the price card and make unilateral and arbitrary decisions about pricing, yet for most consumers price levels are not the key decision maker. Value, or at least perceived value, is a far more potent persuader.

Before the credit crunch of 2008, most families or households had settled on their supermarket of choice on the basis of a number of factors. Of course, convenience is a key factor, as few people will drive several miles to do their *shopping* if it isn't necessary. After all, shopping isn't an emotional issue, is it? Wrong! Shopping is a hugely emotional issue, although the decision process may say something about us which we may find uncomfortable. Pre-2008, every UK supermarket chain had its place in the social hierarchy. People generally accepted that M&S and Waitrose were at the top of the tree – a position endorsed by a widespread awareness that prices were higher and a perception that higher quality was the reward for these prices. Tesco and Sainsbury's were generally perceived to occupy the next level, with Asda and Morrisons in a similar position depending on geography. Lidl and Aldi were considered by many to have less 'class appeal', but now, after the credit crunch has bitten hard in the UK, the fortunes of what may have been perceived as less attractive supermarkets have blossomed while the 'classier' retailers have been struggling and have had to rethink part of their range to offer more apparent value for money. In the end, if economic factors dictate cutting the family's budget, prudent consumers will seek out the best value regardless of other factors.

What does this mean in veterinary terms? In normal economic times, people will comfortably find their own preferred level when choosing a veterinary practice. Even in those circumstances, however, some 20–25% of those pet owners who do use a vet were floating between vets and using more than one practice.[4] When asked why, many responded that they had found it easier to segment what they perceived as 'their' veterinary needs and to use different practices to meet those needs. For many people, products such as flea and worm treatments and cat or dog food were simply commodities, even if they were branded, since the same brands could be bought elsewhere, possibly more conveniently or at a better price. Other people found it easier to register the animals (if required) and to collect the product from a practice close to work or on the way to or from the school, football club or station. When the dog needed attention, some consumers preferred one practice, while their cat seemed to prefer a vet in another practice and, when it came to wanting a diagnosis for something which was suspected to be serious or needing more complex surgery, many pet owners had definite preferences which might involve using a number of practices.

In one case, a practitioner believed he had a large number of 'bonded' clients, judging by the number of animals he vaccinated and believing the industry mantra that vaccination signals a lasting relationship. He was horrified to find that his 'bonded' clients were using him for vaccinations because he was cheaper and they perceived vaccination as a commodity, while being registered for *emotional* all other veterinary work at another practice nearby. What to one of us is an *emotional* bond may be no more than a pragmatic decision to someone else, as I found out when one pet owner I was interviewing listed 'euthanasia' as a commodity that could be bought anywhere.

LINKING THE MARKET TO CONSUMER BEHAVIOUR

Every culture is different, but in Western Europe we are in some ways closest to US patterns of consumer behaviour. This grouping conventionally also includes Australasia and other nations with a substantial European population, although in economic terms the group would normally be restricted to nations with a high average annual income per capita.[5] As a result, we demonstrate highly developed skills in decision making. In our culture we have no need to haggle, and if a price and level of service is set we are highly adept at making rapid yet considered decisions based on something else which we can only describe as perceived value. Even in times of comparative plenty, we are price conscious, but that doesn't stop at the bald figures stating the price of something. We have become skilled at taking into consideration a wide range of factors, such as convenience in terms of car parking, location, traffic density and opening hours to suit our needs. We are swayed by added value, such as free gifts, the free servicing of equipment or extended guarantees at little or no extra cost, and in a retail environment we are always influenced by the personality of the salesperson, despite our protestations to the contrary. While we are accustomed to making decisions, often based on fine distinctions, between similar brands, we are also easily swayed by the personalities of certain brands and the styles in which they are portrayed and displayed. If we like a brand, we want to like the people who recommend it, because, deep down, we see that we are similar people and feel a degree of unconscious familiarity with the process.

In many cases, our brand loyalty is a highly sophisticated process built up over a long period of

time or by a series of experiences, and we hope and expect these brands to develop and mature alongside our continuing support. When a setback occurs, sufficient to shake or sever such brand loyalty, the shock effect is almost palpable and we experience a pang of genuine disappointment. Psychologists might say that this *disappointment* is inward looking and reflects *dissatisfaction* with ourselves for having made the choice or having stuck to it despite evidence that it was misguided.

disappointment, dissatisfaction

Our culture is highly adept at shopping and even sees it as recreational. What else but a consumer society could find window shopping enjoyable? But of course we do window shopping unconsciously. Driving down the street, if we are pet owners, we may see a sign for a new boarding kennel opening soon; we will mentally file that away in case we need it later in the year. If we see a sign for a new veterinary practice opening soon, we will make a rapid mental calculation to determine our level of satisfaction with our current veterinary arrangements and compare it with our level of curiosity about the new service. If our existing relationship is unsatisfactory, the visual cue to bring a new service into play might be sufficient for us to determine to give it a try. If our last experience was faintly disappointing, the likelihood of our changing to the new one is in direct proportion to how deeply we feel bonded to the existing practice, how good our previous experiences have been, how comfortable we have felt with the existing arrangement and for how long. This is a complex set of comparisons, yet we will make it in a fraction of a second and will either accept the new proposition for immediate or stored action or, alternatively, reject the proposition altogether. Each time we test our commitment to the existing practice, we either reinforce or erode the relationship entirely unconsciously.

Textbooks would describe the importance we accord to our relationship with pets as a distinctive feature of North American and European communities. While the pet is well, expenditure on it, or consumption of products and services, is a pleasurable exercise. The growth of the '*pet pound*' in the UK, encompassing purchases made through supermarkets, pet stores, groomers and other outlets, is staggering: growth far exceeds the veterinary surgeon's wildest dreams. As an example, the AN online pet superstore has managed to grow its turnover by £2m in the last year, as pet owners turn increasingly to the Internet, and has now received additional investment to help it expand.[6] UK consumer expenditure on pet food and pet care products per animal increased by a robust 5.1% in 2006. Moreover, despite the slow increase in the population of cats and dogs, value sales growth accelerated to approach 6% during 2007, as driving market trends continued to hold sway.[7] Sales growth in pet products hit double digits in supermarkets over the same period.

pet pound

During the period 2007–2008, the UK pet insurance market continued to experience strong growth in premium income and policy numbers. There is a positive correlation between household income and the uptake of a pet insurance policy, with the propensity to take up pet insurance increasing with household income. Product penetration was highest among consumers with a household income above £50,000,[8] yet when animals fall sick it is often the households with lowest incomes that most need pet insurance. This aptly highlights the antithetical nature of the veterinary practice business.

On the one hand, when things are going well, despite rational arguments for a veterinary

surgeon being the best person to sell flea or worm treatments, food or other pet paraphernalia to pet owners, competition is very stiff and consumers gravitate towards 'happier' sales outlets without medical connotations to buy these goods. When the economy is in trouble, price pressures are strongest and drive more sales through one-stop outlets such as supermarkets or pet superstores.

When the animal is sick or injured, however, this is not the time for what the Americans call 'experiential consumption' but is instead a time for *distress purchases*. At this point, normal consumer behaviour switches off and naked *emotion* surfaces. The vet, instead of being a mere retailer, becomes a medical expert with the diagnostic skills and experience to save the day. In the consumer's eyes, all vets are adequately/suitably/equally qualified and all walk on water. The point of differentiation then becomes not cost but confidence. As long as the consumer has confidence in the veterinary surgeon or the practice as a whole, cost is a lesser consideration and other reinforcers of the consumer's decision to hand their pet's life to that particular vet or practice kick in. The process is just as unconscious as normal consumer behaviour and is made in the same fashion, but with different factors coming into play. There is no thought of loyalty programmes, extended guarantees or even convenience here. The only thing that matters is the outcome, and pet owners will happily put up with being spoken to in a brusque manner which they will put down to professional attitude in this instance but wouldn't tolerate in the context of experiential consumption.

The bald truth is that everything is just fine for the fire-brigade side of veterinary practice. As long as consumers have faith and confidence, when the need is for diagnostic skills and clinical intervention the practice should do well and should be able to charge realistically, even if it is more expensive than some competitors. It is only after the event, when the pet is repaired and healthy again, that the normal consumer attitude and decision-making process resurfaces.

REFERENCES

1 S. Bellman, G. Lohse and E.J. Johnson, 'Predictors of Online Buying Behavior', *Communications of the ACM*, Vol. 42 (2009), pp. 32–48

2 S. Bellman, G. Lohse and E.J. Johnson, 'Consumer behaviour on the Internet – Findings from panel data', *Journal of Interactive Marketing*, Vol. 14, No. 1 (2000), pp. 15–29

3 Workplace Employee Relations Survey 1998

4 R. Tiffin, 'Mind the gap', talk on behalf of Onswitch Insight; VPMA Congress 2005

5 E. Arnould, L. Price and G. Zinkhan, *Consumers*, 2nd edition; McGraw-Hill, 2004

6 C. Knox, 'Growth as pet owners go online', *The Journal* 27 February 2009 (www.nebusiness.co.uk/business-news/latest-business-news/2009/02/27/)

7 Euromonitor press release 'Going upmarket: Premiumisation driving UK pet care industry', September 2007 (www.majormarketprofiles.com/press.aspx)

8 Datamonitor report 'UK Pet Insurance 2009' (www.datamonitor.com/store/Product/uk_pet_insurance_2009?productid=DMFS2418)

CHAPTER V
How consumers think

How consumers think

You're inside my head
Inside my head

Whatever you really said to him?
Is sitting there, inside of me

And you bother me
You possess me
You're there again
Ahead of me
And I won't let go
I won't let go

You're inside my head

Radiohead

CUSTOMERS VERSUS CONSUMERS

customers

Many excellent books encouraging business people to perform better advise them to think like their *customers*. Some are quite explicit in suggesting that we should think about the same things as our customers, but such advice can only work where one is selling products or services to people who all share a similar role, such as accountants, financial executives or fashion buyers. It is far less likely to work in the field of small-animal veterinary services, where our consumers have a variety of backgrounds and experience, although it would be useful advice for those employed in large-animal work.

As a matter of fact, just what do our consumers think about while they're sitting waiting to be attended to? Again, we would need to segment them into those who are attending for a 'distress purchase', because their pet is sick, and those who have come for a happier reason, possibly hoping to ensure that their pet doesn't get sick. What we love to label as 'preventative care' is, to the cat or dog owner, only about making sure that their Fluffy stays healthy, happy and beautiful.

So, while they are sitting there, why aren't our consumers summoning their thoughts about presenting symptoms: the fact that Fluffy was limping a week last Thursday or the colour of his stools? These are, after all, highly significant clues for the veterinary surgeon's lonely task of detection and diagnosis. For the pet owner, however, they are only significant if he or she has the experience to put them into context and form a suspicion of a diagnosis, and in reality practitioners prefer to arrive at their own diagnosis.

Which hat will consumers be wearing when they come into the surgery? Unless there's clear evidence of pain and distress, sufficient to generate enough concern to crowd out any other considerations, our consumers will be acting as humans first and pet owners second. This means that each consumer will, just like you and me, have twenty unanswered emails and three messages on their phone to deal with. Each one of them will be processing data about something else planned for later that day, the children's tea, who has which dental appointment, whether or not there are sufficient funds left on the credit card at this stage in the month and whether or not they locked the front door. Because our lives are so filled with information and because so much of it is ephemeral, our normal consumer behaviour tends to concentrate on the ephemera but to hold the data in the transit lounge of our brains, from which it can simply be deleted once deemed to have served its purpose.

short-term storage

Unless we have a strong reason to do otherwise, we all process mountains of data by consigning it to very *short-term storage* and looking at the headlines only, rather than digging deep into the text to find out a lot of supporting information. We don't do that routinely because our experience shows that we don't need that information routinely. How many times have you forgotten the name of someone you're introduced to before you've even let go of their hand? That's partly down to our laziness and partly because we recognise that, as a rule, we aren't going to need that information again and so it's not worth storing it ready for recall. So much information and so little time!

As a rule, we now receive more information in a day than our forebears did in a month or even

longer. We receive information from every quarter: from TV and radio, from the telephones we carry, from advertising hoardings, from friends and neighbours, from clients and suppliers – the list is endless. Additionally, when we drive our cars, we receive information about the world through our eyes, our ears and the other sensory organs which we take for granted. At the same time, we are receiving crucial data about the car and the whole driving process through our eyes and ears, but also through our fingertips, the soles of our feet and the sides and backs of our seats. If it's raining or sunny, if the traffic is heavy or there are children about, we have even more data to process.

Then there's the issue of time. Some of us wear watches while others can manage without, but there isn't a waking moment in the day when we aren't conscious of time and the relationship between actual time and our planned use of it. Additionally, for many of us, while we're asleep and unaware of time ticking away in the background, our subconscious is still processing the data, enabling most of us to wake up at the allotted time without the use of an alarm clock. And on top of all this there are the pressures associated with work – or, for some, the lack of it. Is it any wonder that our brains feel overloaded and that we operate on autopilot much of the time?

If we can accept that our consumers, whether we know them by sight or not, won't enter the premises armed with the conscious thought processes which we might hope for, then we are making headway. Too many vets seem to expect the presenting pet's owner to be ready with razor-sharp answers to all our questions. In the absence of the obvious stimuli of blood, broken bones or other signs of distress, the vast majority of presenting people will have something else on their minds as they sit waiting. Clearly, we don't need to think about the same things – an impossible goal in any case – but we do need to recognise that the information we are about to impart will be received into the same transit lounge in their heads as the gas bills and the kids' dental appointments, unless we flag up something of real significance.

In business, we learn quite early on that a sales pitch filled with lurid detail of who we are and what we do is of almost zero significance to those we are talking to. In truth, they are usually far more interested in themselves, who they are and what they do, so it's far more profitable for us to talk about what we have learned about them – assuming it's repeatable!

Following this advice, what do we actually know about the consumers who present with their pets? The terms 'consumer' and 'client' or 'customer' are often considered to be interchangeable, but I'm firmly of the view that, in our practice, once the person and/or the pet is on the premises and seeking advice, we are dealing with consumers and not customers. The definition of each word is subtly different, but there's so much hidden in that subtlety!

A customer is defined as an individual or an organisation who buys a product or service; a consumer is the person who uses the product or service or may be affected by its purchase.[1]

One could argue that, in the veterinary field, the customer and the consumer are sometimes the same person, but there are some more recent considerations that affect how both operate.

If we assume that consumers already know what outcome they want from the transaction and that they operate in customer mode when they choose from the array of options that the practice offers them, that is a trifle simplistic, because the consumer has grown in recent years. Growth in confidence, in the desire to be recognised as an equal in the decision-making process and in the absolute certainty that consumers can always find another supplier has made the twenty-first-century consumer a very different animal from yesterday's 'bonded client'. The overriding caveat here is that we need to separate the occasions when the consumer is coming in for preventative treatment, general advice, pet food or microchipping from the occasions when there is clear concern, or mounting panic, about their pet's health or prognosis.

In these latter situations, the relationship can be utterly different. If the process of diagnosis and treatment goes well, the normal consumer thought processes of weighing up the pros and cons, with the necessary reinforcement feedback from the environment in which the process is taking place, in order to assess the success and rewarding nature of the transaction and make an informed decision will go into abeyance. If things don't go well, however, or if the interpersonal relationship on which the initial trust was based should deteriorate, then normal consumer decision making may be brought back into play, the animal may be removed from the practice's care, or frank and overt criticism may ensue.

The critical issue here is *trust*, and this is what differentiates a veterinary practice as a retailer of products and services from other retailers. There's no need for any element of trust in the retailer, nor is any sought, when a consumer is purchasing a branded commodity such as pet food or a flea or worm treatment, if the branded product already has 'trust' embedded in the DNA of its brand values. If a consumer wants 'I ❤ K9' dog food because the brand values are reproducible wherever it is purchased, the place of purchase will be determined by factors other than retailer trust. Service, convenience or price are far more likely persuaders.

trust

This is the basic premise of the currently spreading trend for the 25% or so of pet owners who do use a vet to use more than one veterinary practice. The practice they choose for buying branded commodities may well be different from the practice they trust to diagnose a serious condition or again to treat an RTA. The development of and rapid growth in the pet health segment of other retail channels, such as pet or grocery, is testament to the British consumer's trust in the power of brands.

Customers' concern with value is proved by the lengths that major supermarket chains go to in order to discourage their customers from buying the same branded goods elsewhere. Here again we see the merging of consumers and customers. The consumer part of the individual's brain will select the brands and presentations that he or she wishes to buy, and the customer part of the process will decide whether to buy these same goods at Tesco or the corner shop, largely on the basis of convenience. It's only when the decision to transfer the family's shopping *loyalty* from Tesco to Sainsbury's is taken that the consumer part of the individual's brain reverts to assessing the pros and cons to ensure that a satisfying and rewarding choice is finally made. The challenge for the supermarkets is to persuade purchasers that consumer values need to be brought into play and that there really would be some benefit in that individual developing a form of loyalty to that brand of

loyalty

brand perception supermarket. The hierarchy of *brand perception* is fascinating and would fill a separate book.

In my own family, we have little real commitment to any brand of supermarket, but an offer of 5 pence a litre off petrol is enough for me to commit to using that particular retailer until the offer ends. What does that say about me? I suppose it says that I'm easily bribed, but that's the whole point of consumerism: like countless others, when I make a decision about purchasing something I want to feel that I made the right decision. The lure of 5 pence a litre off fuel is sufficient to tip my loyalty, just for the duration of the offer. Clearly, I'm not making the decision on brand values, as I only buy branded goods that are easily available everywhere else. If I rode a moped a couple of thousand miles a year, the offer wouldn't be so tempting, but as I drive at least 35,000 miles a year, it is far more meaningful to me. So it isn't the offer itself but the context into which the consumer puts the offer that really matters.

In the veterinary context, a practice in the middle of a new-build estate full of young children will generate more consumer interest with an attractive initial vaccination offer for all those young puppies and kittens than it will with budget senior health checks. Staying open until 11 pm every night may not generate additional income if there are plenty of young mothers around all day caring for small children. Conversely, discounted microchipping at midday will not help if the practice's consumer base is at work in London during the day.

DO CONSUMERS THINK AT ALL?

total customer value Most businesses now strive to offer a 'total customer value' product or service which holds the consumer at its focus and recognises that modern consumers, whether they are buying goods or services, will attach a series of values to whatever they buy. Increasingly, retailers are coming to accept that capturing a consumer for a lifetime is an opportunity far too valuable to miss, and so the idea that a quality relationship starts with the consumer him- or herself and not with the product is widely accepted, even though it is seldom achieved. Many retailers' marketing departments espouse the added value of seeking to make consumers' lives easier, only to find that the whole process has been undermined by an awkward or inattentive salesperson. Suppose I were to buy a new car: I know exactly what I would want that car to do for me and I could make the decision about the car itself quite quickly. If I had to shop around to find a dealer who would throw in an extra year's warranty or two years' free servicing, that would be when my consumer experience would kick in and I'd be clicking my mouse feverishly to find the best offer. If I then had to drive four hundred miles to collect the car because the retailer wouldn't deliver it, that would affect my decision making, just as it would if another dealer would only supply my car in lime-green metallic paint. My first objection would be rational and purely based on convenience; the second would be deeply rooted in my psyche subconscious and in all the insecurities which would appear unbidden in my *subconscious* brain. One rational decision, one irrational, and both made within a nanosecond of processing time.

Did I think about it? No.

Was this typical consumer processing of data? Yes.

So understanding who the consumer is, how they spend their money and what is important to them are all of interest to the organisation or individual trying to sell to them, but it is also important to understand who and what affects or influences their decision to purchase or repurchase. Chapter 7 looks at such influences in detail, but it's worth mentioning at this stage the concept of '*decision-making units*', which can very often be the family as a whole, or one or more members of the family. In some cases, one member of the family may hold the purse strings and any purchasing decision will additionally have to be signed off by that person before it can proceed. In other cases, the principal influence may be the children and, for a large number of reasons, purchasing decisions may start or end with the children.

decision-making units

Society is constantly changing, and many societal changes can be seen to be the result of socioeconomic developments. For instance, in the UK we have a rising *population*, currently standing at 60,975,000. More and more people are now living singly in the UK[2] and, as a result of people living longer, healthier lives, we also have an older generation which is comparatively fit and active and now represents some 20% of the population, as do children under the age of 16. We also have more divorced families, many of whose children now have more influence and tangential buying power than ever before. So there are more aspects to each family and more points of influence, and this influence can often be spread over a large geographic area.

population

In 2001, around 8% of the population was born overseas, a figure more than double that for 1951, and with the recent influx of workers from Eastern Europe the figure will now be higher still. As a result, we are seeing significant changes in the types of people making up the 'consumer' group.

Within the UK, 33% of the 25.3 million households live within 3% of the land available and 50% own 94% of the wealth, leaving the remaining 50% to share just 6% of the wealth between them.

So people come from hugely disparate backgrounds, have greatly differing access to wealth and opportunity and have vastly different expectations. To lump everyone together under the term 'consumers' is clearly a nonsense unless each consumer is viewed as an individual. This is all the more important when we consider that around 11% of the UK population moves home in a typical year: added to the floating 25% plus who use more than one practice, this mobility produces a significant churn in the consumer base available to each practice.

Some things are consistent, however, and in most communities the influences on *purchasing behaviour* revolve around friends and family, commercial input (i.e. advertising and retailers), and mass media (i.e. magazines, newspapers, TV and radio). There is also a final category, 'experience', which plays a massive part, both positive and negative, in influencing purchasing decisions.

purchasing behaviour

All of these factors contribute to the '*evaluation*' *stage* of the purchasing decision, and some are accorded more importance than others. As an example, an individual may be influenced by advertising to purchase a flea product from a supermarket, having never tried it before. If it fails to work, the cost is fairly insignificant and it is likely that advice will be sought from a more dependable source, in the form of friends and family. That recommendation might be considered more thoroughly than the first because of the earlier failure, but because the source of recommendation

'evaluation' stage

will be considered to be more authoritative, it will in turn make the next decision easier. The process is achieved by a series of unconscious assessments and rapid thought processes which add up to an invisible spreadsheet of pros and cons, all contributing to a purchasing decision.

In many cases, previous experience with a quality branded item will make the process quick and easy, but if the consumer is trying to save money or to avoid going to the retailer who sold the effective branded item, other factors will come into play. Each influence is accorded an imaginary weight, with some being more influential than others, and the spreadsheet is then considered as a whole. If only it were that simple! We have come a long way from bartering apples in our local village, and consumer behaviour today is a complex mix of market observations tempered by an inner desire to 'get it right' for deeply personal reasons. For some people, the deep need to avoid the problems caused by 'getting it wrong' is at least as powerful a driver as the desire for a successful transaction.

Consumer decision making can have several phases or the process can be rapid and decisive. There are also different types of purchasing decisions, ranging from 'routine' to 'corrective'. Routine decisions often relate to uncomplicated purchases such as petrol or newspapers. These are often commodities but this type of decision can also be applied to low-risk purchasing where a trusted brand of goods is required.

Of course, if the consumer seeks to buy branded goods at the best price, this is a very different proposition from finding and then buying a better treatment for their dog's fleas. It may difficult for the consumer to make such a decision without additional information or endorsement, and these 'complex' decisions are often seen as carrying a higher risk of failure and dissatisfaction. They may involve purchases of a higher value, thus increasing the risk, or in an area where the consumer has little or no background knowledge. The higher the perceived risk, the higher will be the requirement for an authoritative endorsement or information from a reliable source.

Sadly, not everyone believes that the vet is the best source of information about pet health. In a recent survey, 63% of those surveyed preferred other sources of information for advice about pets in general and a staggering 33% chose other sources than the vet for advice about their pets' health. Long gone are the days when the public held professionals in awe and respect for their knowledge.

When consumers need to supplement their own understanding in order to correct a previously unsatisfactory decision, this *'corrective' decision* is important because it carries with it the underlying fear of dissatisfaction and the risk of compounding both a financial and a practical mistake. It is likely that the process this time will take longer and will involve more sources of information and stronger levels of support. Although it may not be any more discernible on the surface, this process will involve the consumer in making greater efforts, so as to be as sure as possible of avoiding a further mistake. In the final analysis, each of us is comfortable with a different level of emotion being brought to bear on the process. Some of us are more considered and will research things thoroughly; others are far more emotional and will accept advice and act on it precipitously. It comes down to our personal characteristics and what kind of consumer we are.

Of course, nothing is straightforward. While the process of making the decision itself is complex enough, consumers add to the agony by going through a mental process of evaluation after

'corrective' decision

cognitive dissonance

the purchase, seeking reassurance that they made the correct decision. This is designed to avoid a mental state known as 'cognitive dissonance', which arises when, post-purchase, the consumer feels that some aspects of the transaction were not correct or satisfying. Cognitive dissonance can lead to a far more complex process when a subsequent purchase becomes necessary.

In the UK we are very adept at showing our displeasure by voting with our feet and refusing to return to a retailer, restaurant or other establishment. These tiny acts of consumerist triumph are immensely satisfying for a brief moment but do not allow us any closure, or any mechanism for coming to terms with the failed transaction. From a consumer's point of view, this may be seen as a poor result that can still lead to a satisfying alternative purchase, but from the retailer's perspective it is hugely complicating, as they may never hear from that consumer again and will rarely, if ever, find out the cause of the dissatisfaction. Of course, the post-purchase evaluation phase is as important to the retailer as it is to the consumer, but it is well recognised that very few businesses

customer satisfaction

ever follow up transactions to measure *customer satisfaction*. Almost all companies spend four to five times as much on seeking new customers as they do on retaining existing ones, despite the fact that this approach also costs them dearly in lost customers.

The other day, I saw a mobile phone provider's advertisement offering a really attractive deal to new customers, but no such deal was available to me, as a loyal customer for the last four years. I phoned them, but was told that I couldn't have the same deal, so I promptly changed providers to take advantage of a different deal, which probably wasn't available to long-term supporters of that provider either. Consumers are fickle creatures and their purchasing decisions are largely based on emotional factors, not on logic. Above all, consumers' decisions will reflect their individual personality type, and this guides us in charting what type of consumer each of us is.

REFERENCES

1 I. Doole, P. Lancaster and R. Lowe, *Understanding and managing customers*; FT Prentice Hall, 2004
2 UK Office for National Statistics 2007

CHAPTER VI
The concepts of 'self' and personality

The concepts of 'self' and personality

Because I realised I got
me myself and
that's all I got in the end
that's what I found out
and it ain't no need to cry
I took a vow that from now on
I'm gonna be my own best friend

Beyonce

VI

SELF AND OUTSIDE FORCES

Understanding the concept of 'self' and the ways in which the 'self' interacts with other *social constructs*, in relationships with individuals and with other organisations, is an essential foundation for gaining insight into consumer behaviour. If only it were easy to do!

We should all be able to identify the factors that make up our own, individual concept of 'self': the cultural overlay that has dominated our upbringing, whether that be one of class, creed, colour or confidence; the ways in which we have individually sought to define ourselves, by our interests, our age group, our career or the social tribe we belong to or aspire to; and how our 'self'-concept affects all the social processes of interaction with others and interpersonal influences on others, within or without our circle of influence. Yet, while we recognise that we should each be capable of identifying what makes up our own blueprint of 'self', most of us would struggle to articulate these factors. When asked to talk about ourselves in an interview, for instance, we will often opt for a slightly self-deprecating description, as if we were keen to avoid boasting about ourselves. Just as many of us 'see' a different image of ourselves from that observed by others, we will often struggle to make an accurate list of our attributes, unless they are recognised as factual data, such as schooling, qualifications and work experience.

What is more, in so many social situations, people will amend the truth slightly to make the report they give about themselves better fit their notion of what others may be expecting. In so many ways, most of us seek – whether consciously or unconsciously – to fit in with the chosen group, whether that is a collection of neighbours, work colleagues, friends or family. As a result, the perception that we have of ourselves may be different from the reality.

That statement should give the reader an inkling of the difficulties to come in this chapter, as it must be clear that there are as many variations on the theme of 'self' as there are individuals to consider, and yet an understanding of the relationship between people's concepts of 'self' and their consumption behaviour is key to understanding how and why people behave in the way they do.

What is 'self'?

In essence, the concept of 'self' is a convenient way for us to package our understanding of the aims and aspirations of individuals. Arnould, Price and Zinkhan[1] describe the concept of 'self' as 'an organised configuration of perceptions of the self, which are available to awareness'. In other words, they say that self-concepts are perceptions that people have about themselves.

In the real world, each and every one of us now interacts with a hundred or even a thousand times the number of people that our medieval ancestors did, and we tend to think in terms of relationships with two different groups. The first consists of those who affect our lives emotionally or through some other form of control: family, loved ones, special friends, immediate colleagues at work and people with whom we share an active interest in either a work or a leisure environment – these we might term 'significant others'. The second, far larger group consists of acquaintances with no special links, people whom we feel comfortable to exclude from any considerations about our

'self' or inner thoughts. It is clear, then, that 'self' cannot operate in isolation and that it is not separable from our personal society and our culture.

Our sense of 'self' grows out of our interactions with others within our environment but is hardly influenced by actions and activities that take place outside our environment. Hence, in general terms, we may respond emotionally to appeals help victims of famine in far-flung places and feel comfortable in assuaging our transient concern by donating money to aid these people, but because they operate outside our immediate sphere we are able to dismiss them from our thoughts with scarcely a backward glance. On the other hand, the distress of someone within our immediate environment prompts a different response because, directly or indirectly, it impinges on our own concept of 'self'. Whether this latter situation engenders our engagement because of a genuine concern for the individual(s) concerned or because we feel that a certain response is required by our cultural overlay and our desire to be seen to have behaved in a 'proper' fashion is a topic far greater than the reach of this chapter, but both motives coexist in most people's lives within the cultural norm of Western society.

As an example, when we go to view a house that we are considering buying, we might make an immediate decision, on reaching the garden gate, that we have made a mistake and this house is not for us. The behavioural norm, however, requires us to go through a charade of proceeding with the viewing and pretending that we are interested, because it is impolite to seem critical of others' tastes in furnishing or living style if it's different from our own. Isn't that stupid? It wastes everyone's time, gives unfounded hope to the vendors and serves only to lengthen the entire process, but in accepting the invitation to visit someone else's home we have temporarily become part of a new and different tribe and feel the need to treat these complete strangers as if they were part of our own circle of significant others, with the same attendant courtesies and social behaviours.

What influences this idea of 'self'?

The sense of 'self' is developed through interactions with three aspects of our immediate environment:

- individuals who are important to us, whether through transient or longer-term relationships
- the physical environment of objects and material possessions that affect us, sometimes to the point of defining us
- values and beliefs – even ideologies – which influence the way in which we interact within our environment.

These three influences shouldn't be seen as somehow stand-alone and independent of each other, as there are frequently strong links between all three. Take, as an example, the concept of 'keeping up with the Joneses'. We are all familiar with this, as an extension to the concept of being defined by what you wear, what you say and what you spend your money on, and this concept has been fundamental to the growth of advertising over the last fifty years. Some decades ago, a popular advertisement for a tobacco product claimed that 'You're never alone with a "Strand"', a message designed to engender a sense of belonging and camaraderie between purchasers of these cigarettes.

Did people buy the product because they liked it more than other cigarettes or because it gave them a sense of belonging? In either case, the desire to consume that brand became a building block in the development of 'self' in those smokers who were already partly defined by their feeling of kinship with other smokers.

If a group of families all live in otherwise identical houses, it is not uncommon for one family to set a trend of home improvement. with new windows or perhaps a new porch or kitchen. Within weeks, every house in that group has enjoyed or endured some 'improvement'. as each family seeks to define its position as being either of like mind or having the need to exceed the others' achievements. For some, the drive will be to demonstrate that they are players in what they perceive to be a desirable social group, which could also be construed as a desire not to be left behind, while for others the drive will be to be the top dog by demonstrating better taste, more cash or whatever values they consider to be defining of their own sense of 'self' as perceived by others.

One wonders whether in times of comparative economic hardship these values and the conspicuous display of wealth will temporarily become a social taboo rather than a demonstration of one-upmanship. This would, however, depend on a mass migration of social values within a complete social group effecting a form of transition. Normally, to produce such a change would require a major change in any of the three influencing elements – the individuals, the material environment or the cultural influences – and a global economic recession might prove to be just the sort of event to effect widespread change in what defines people individually or en masse. Such a change is known as 'role transition' or a major change in the rights, duties and responsibilities *role transition* expected of an individual by a social group.[2] As the examples above illustrate, role transitions can be expected to influence people's purchasing or consumption behaviour.

Can we observe and measure 'self'?

How can we measure this concept of 'self' and relate it to the behaviour of consumers? A term that most of us are more familiar with is 'personality', and this is a traditional construct for describing 'self' either in ourselves or in others. It's obvious that we are all different, even though for most of our lives we may clamour to be seen as belonging to identifiable groups. Listen to a group of people discussing something amusing and it's easy to identify individuals by their type of laughter, the cadence of their speech and other ways in which they behave within the group. They may be sharing a common topic of discussion but their personalities are defined by the ways in which they interact within their environment and with significant others. Psychologists use a series of principles to analyse such behaviour, including motivation, attitude and learning, in an attempt to understand how consumers respond to brands and to purchasing or consumption opportunities and to identify like-minded categories of consumers.

In short, the way we perceive our environment, our learning experiences, our conscious and unconscious influences and how we interact within that environment all combine to shape our individual personality. However, even if someone is typically referred to as laconic or dour, that person may not always behave in the predicted way. So if, for instance, someone is short-changed in *emotion* a shop, their expected reaction might have been to make a sarcastic observation, yet on occasion they may react in a way that suggests a different set of *emotions*, such as anger or feelings of victimisation. Nevertheless, it is clear that, while individuals can be influenced by a wide range of events and other people, giving rise to unpredictable behaviour, in the main personality tends to remain more or less constant over long periods of time, probably a lifetime, with small changes engendered by significant events or influences. In essence, personality can be summed up as an aggregate of behavioural characteristics that remain largely similar over time.

Clearly, how we feel about ourselves will be a major influence on the development of our personality. Some aspects of personality will be shaped by genetics,[3] such as certain forms of depression and anxiety, although so much of personality will be formulated during the first years of life by contact with parents, siblings or family members that it can be difficult to isolate the principal influences on early personality development. People may have an inherited predisposition to behave in certain ways, which could include a talent for music, art or sport,[4] but there are so many influences on personality that, despite much research, it is impossible to devise a convenient list.

Categorising personality types

Galen In the second century AD, the Greek philosopher *Galen* believed that personalities were of four main types:

- choleric – violent, irritable or aggressive
- sanguine – passionate, cheerful
- melancholic – gloomy, miserable or depressive
- phlegmatic – distant, cold or calm.

This theory was based on the combination of fluids within the body, such as blood, bile or phlegm, that a person was supposed to have been born with. While Galen's theory hasn't survived the passage of time, his four major categories of temperament are still recognisable as the precursors of modern theories of personality traits. The language may have changed, but his observations of types of personality have remained in common everyday use.

Sheldon The American psychologist William *Sheldon* proposed something not dissimilar in the twentieth century, with his classification of personality through body shapes. Sheldon's theory was that there were three different types of body shape and that each could be associated with a different personality. Hence:

- endomorphs, being round and fat, would be easy going, non-aggressive and would love food
- mesomorphs would be strong and muscular, and as a result would be assertive, active and extrovert
- ectomorphs, with their thin, weedy shape, would naturally be introverted, socially inhibited, perhaps intellectual and often loners.

Just like astrology and phrenology, this association of personality with some outward observation, linking people's personalities with stereotypical values, suffers from being overly simplistic. Sheldon's theory has little validity today, other than to familiarise us with the three

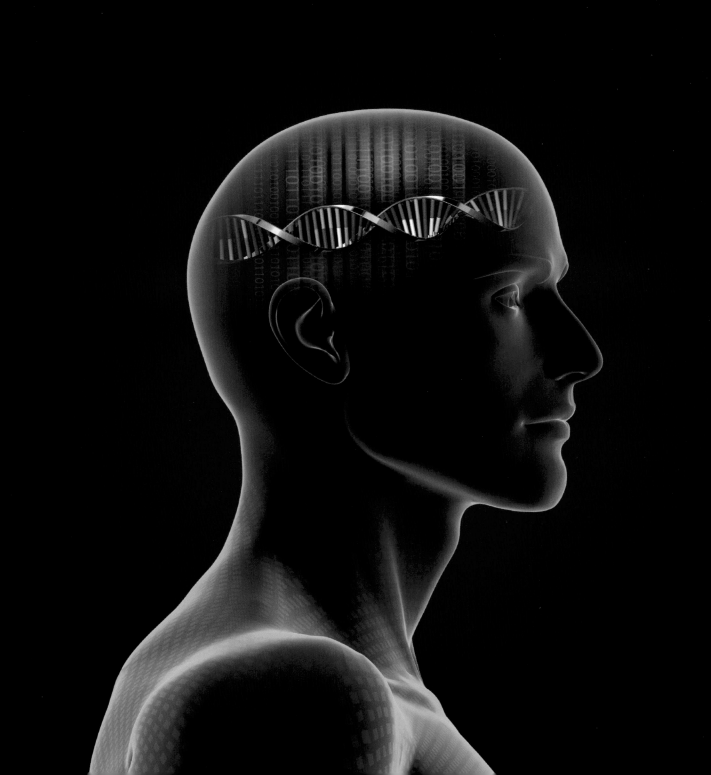

descriptions of body type. Intriguingly, we still like to think of fat, round people as being jolly and muscular and well-built people as being sporty, while if we picture an intellectual or nerd we often picture a thin, inhibited person with glasses. But folklore and reality often clash: at the finishing line of a recent half-marathon, the fastest times – recorded by the fittest and most athletic contestants – were set by the thin, wiry runners; and when the fatter contestants arrived, somewhat later, they didn't seem anything like as jolly.

Gall
Aristotle
Over the years there have been many attempts to identify personality types with some manifestation of people's outward appearance, ranging from *Gall*'s theory of bumps on the head and *Aristotle*'s theories of physiognomy to Lombroso's theory that a tendency towards criminal behaviour could be identified from the structure of the head and face. None of these has stood the test of time, yet some facial types are still considered today to be a guide to an aberrant personality or potential criminal behaviour. How often have we heard someone say 'He looks guilty'?

Our popular culture is still confused and sends out conflicting messages. In Western society, a fat woman may be seen as overly sedentary, possibly belonging to a poor socio-demographic group and even, perhaps, having a preference for fatty fast food. In many people's view, she probably lacks of education. In many parts of India, by contrast, a surplus of body fat can be seen as a badge of attainment or of comparative wealth, as many people would simply not have the economic resources to achieve obesity.

Personality – types and traits

Personality traits
Personality traits are characteristics whereby one person will differ from another in a consistent way. Hence personality traits are different from types of personality.

personality types
In *personality types*, general similarities in personality are gathered together as a convenient way of categorising groups of people whose behaviour might be predicted to be similar. Personality types are really too simplistic a description of human personality, whereas personality traits are, according to the psychologist Gordon *Allport*, the building blocks of personality – 'Traits, on the contrary, are considered wholly within the compass of the individual' [5] – and could perhaps be regarded as the DNA of individual personality.

Allport
Allport recognised that, while some traits were present to a greater or lesser degree in all people, certain of them, such as ambition or compassion, were more dominant in some people than in others. He also noticed that some traits were far more influential than others in shaping people's lives; in real life, such traits as competitiveness or sexual orientation would be more important in determining a person's personality than, for example, modesty or sensitivity.

He categorised personality traits into four groups:

cardinal traits
- *cardinal traits*: deeply ingrained and the most influential, these can sometimes be obsessive, such as sexual orientation, competitiveness or an appetite for power

central traits
- *central traits*: important (but not all-consuming), such as intelligence, honesty, modesty, humour and compassion

secondary traits
- *secondary traits*: sometimes seen as temporary changes in personality and may only emerge in

certain circumstances; for example, when someone who is normally quiet and reserved becomes loud and excitable after drink or two

■ central and secondary traits reversed: again, in certain circumstances, a central trait and a secondary trait might be reversed, so that a normally extrovert person might become quiet and restrained in an unfamiliar environment.

This work and other studies by psychologists around the world have led, in more recent years, to a simpler classification of personality traits, known as the 'Big Five'. All types of personality should be identifiable using the five-factor model of personality traits drawn up by J.M. Digman in 1990, comprising five factors or dimensions which should apply to each individual:

1 open mind or shut mind
2 conscientious or negligent
3 introvert or extrovert
4 agreeable or hostile
5 emotionally stable or unstable (neuroticism).

If we can identify traits in one individual and compare these to what we find in other individuals, and if we can measure the strength and relevance of each trait, we have the basis of a tool for comparing one individual with another. These five factors are now widely used in the compilation of commercial personality questionnaires, which are used by many businesses to formulate an assessment of personality types.

In commercial terms, it is clear why a company would consider it helpful to know, before employing someone, whether the candidate's outwardly manifested personality traits might make him or her a useful and productive member of the team. In recent years, a whole industry has sprung up to provide guidance in this area for employers and some personal insight for individuals into whether they are suitable candidates for a job. In general terms, this industry sells various forms of psychometric testing, which employs a number of different tools.

psychometric testing

Psychometric testing is an umbrella term for occupational or ability testing and personality profiling. Such tests are typically used to inform selection decisions and/or to understand an individual's career development needs. In both contexts, the tests provide a third-party, detached and independent assessment, in snapshot form, that can enable an employer to make assumptions about a person's suitability for a current or future role within a business.

There are two distinct types of test; the following descriptions of the two categories have been taken from the website of a leading commercial provider of such tests.[6]

occupational testing

■ *Occupational testing:* often known as ability testing. This term is used to describe tests designed to measure the ability and aptitude of candidates, such as verbal reasoning or numeracy. They are often used during assessment centres to inform selection decisions.

personality profiling

■ *Personality profiling* is a method of understanding personality traits and, therefore, the typical behaviours and work-style of an individual. It is typically used to inform selection decisions and/or to understand an individual's career development needs.

Many of us would be intrigued to know what a potential employer might make of us, and few of

us ever have the opportunity to see a completely objective and dispassionate assessment of ourselves. Personality profiling can offer that opportunity, based on our answers to a simple questionnaire, and can be useful for career development. Most of the currently available tests were developed for use in a business setting, and such reports may be useful in that context, but, just as employers need to be trained in the interpretation of these tests, so too should individuals be counselled in the interpretation of any kind of personality test. These tests are ultimately based on the work of psychologists such as Jung, Schwartz, Murray and Eysenck, and for interpretation to be constructive and accurate a deep understanding of the processes involved is required. Any report based on a questionnaire can give rise to problems, even if control questions are built in, as we have a human tendency to subjugate our own reactive emotions and to give answers which we feel may show us in a better light.

Jung, Schwartz, Murray, Eysenck

lifestyle

SELF AND *LIFESTYLE*

We have already touched briefly on the idea that human nature is aspirational. Whether we seek to enjoy the same lifestyle as others, more or better possessions, or more identifiable trappings of whatever we deem to be success, it is normal behaviour for consumers to want something that they don't already have. There is a well-known saying that, to be happy, we should want the things we have rather than have the things we want, but our entire consumer lifestyle is based on aspiring to have something else.

Take a family of two adults with two children: the real needs of that family are somewhere for everyone to sleep, somewhere to cook and eat, and somewhere to relax or do some work. In the past, and in poorer societies today, the whole family could easily be accommodated in one or maybe two rooms. Elizabethan people, unless they were gentry, had little need of a kitchen, as food preparation was minimal and most food would either be eaten cold or cooked in communal ovens, often at the baker's premises. There is a theory that the pizza originated in Naples, where scraps of dough that were no use for baking loaves were cooked with a cheap and plentiful accompaniment – tomatoes – in bakers' ovens and sold to passers-by at an affordable price.

The same Elizabethans had little use for a dining room and most, if not all, of the family would share the same room for sleeping. In today's world we feel the need for each child, wherever possible, to have a separate room, and for a dining room or dining area – although recent statistics show that declining numbers of families regularly eat together at the table. Researchers from the Baylor College of Medicine in Houston surveyed 287 fourth-, fifth- and sixth-graders about their dinner habits for a week[7] and their findings were:

- Children ate 42% of their dinners while watching TV.
- Overweight children ate 50% of their meals in front of the TV, compared with 35% of normal-weight children.
- African-American children consumed 62% of their meals in front of the TV, compared with 43% of Hispanic children, 32% of white children and 21% of Asian-American children.

- Children who ate dinner with their families ate more vegetables and drank fewer sodas than those who ate dinner alone.
- Children who ate with their families were also more likely to eat lower-fat foods such as low-fat milk and salad dressing and lean meats than kids who ate by themselves.

While there are many reasons why we should take family life more seriously, the aspiration to have a separate dining area may not, typically, have its foundations in everyday use. Our example family may aspire to a four-bedroom house that is, if possible, detached in order to minimise contact with other people. More than one bathroom would be desirable, and a multiple garage to store all the children's toys, the golf clubs, the garden furniture and so on. Cars (plural) will be displayed on the drive. In an earlier life, I worked for a Swedish pharmaceutical company in the late 1970s, at a time when inflation was rising rapidly. Many of the salespeople were moving to other companies simply to achieve a pay rise big enough to keep up with inflation. The company's MD solved the problem by giving all those who were entitled to a company car the choice of a Volvo or Saab, instead of the Ford or Vauxhall that they had been offered previously. The exodus stopped immediately, as the perceived social status of a premium-brand car was clearly worth more than cash to the individuals concerned and their families.

The four-bed detached house with multiple garage and two premium cars on the drive is not a necessity for any family, but it is a common aspirational goal. Similarly, owning a holiday home is an aspiration for countless thousands of families. A friend has recently sold a lovely four-bedroom house in Spain, complete with beautifully tended grounds and a sparkling pool. His wife was desolate, but he was relieved: he had done the arithmetic and worked out that the cost of maintaining his second home was so great that he could afford instead to spend four weeks a year with the family in the five-star hotel on the beach which they always visited in Spain. How many weeks a year did they routinely spend in their Spanish holiday home? Three. In the long run, the house had proved to be only modestly successful as an investment, and it had been broken into three times. His approach was undeniably hard-nosed, but his wife's disappointment may perhaps have owed something to the fear that her social standing would be affected by the sale of their second home.

For many of us, our social life is governed by the activities we enjoy doing – whether that be playing golf, fishing, hiking, climbing or cycling, for example. I learned early in life that having shiny new football boots could never improve my performance at left back, but that doesn't stop me aspiring to trade in my elderly Bruce and Walker rod for a Loomis GLX Classic Trout rod and a Hardy Angel reel. I know they won't increase my catch rate, but how good it would feel to hold that rod and reel in my hand! That purely emotional response to a non-existent problem is the essence of our almost global ambition to improve our lifestyle. Whether it is the size of the diamond on your finger, the brand of the watch on your wrist, the car you drive or the designer brand of the clothing you wear to go hiking, it is the human condition to be aspirational and to develop a craving for the outward trappings of our chosen lifestyle.

Most of us only infrequently buy a car, but the volume of sales of the myriad car magazines available suggests that we aren't buying the magazines to research the purchase of a new car.

However interested in the engineering we may be, the love affair that men have with car magazines is a long-term, slow-burn aspirational journey, so that we're ready to make an instant decision as soon as the lottery win is announced. Nor is the involvement of 'self' in the development of a lifestyle limited to the acquisition or consumption of branded goods to be displayed to others, like the courting plumage of a bird. Sometimes, albeit rarely, it is enough to own something even if it must be kept secret, and there are collectors of rare or illegal objects for whom the secret joy of ownership is sufficient.

Another kind of improvement in lifestyle can be the regaining of something which had previously been lost, and the launch of Pfizer's Viagra is a classic case of creative marketing to a significant but unsung market. Before Viagra, men who suffered from impotence had little choice but to grin and bear it, so to speak. When Viagra was brought to market, it was recognised that male impotence was an unromantic disaster for all concerned and that many sufferers were unprepared even to admit to the condition's existence. Pfizer reinvented the condition as erectile dysfunction and provided an answer in the shape of little blue pills containing sildenafil citrate. The combination of the new description of the condition, which sounded far more modern and carried no social stigma, the promotion of the drug Viagra as part of an upmarket, aspirational lifestyle, and the endorsement of high-profile celebrities such as Bob Dole and Pele – all advertised frequently and directly to consumers on prime-time TV – created massive demand. People whose condition had previously been unknown to anyone but their partner and their doctor came forward to create a new and enormous market sector. Not only was the new category of drug was a runaway success for Viagra and all the other products that offered a similar benefit, the effect on society was astonishing. The Viagra brand has become so well known that many fake aphrodisiacs now call themselves 'herbal Viagra' or are presented as blue tablets imitating the shape and colour of Pfizer's product. Viagra is also known informally as 'Vitamin V' and 'the Blue Pill', as well as by various other nicknames.[8]

Indicators of the very strong link between 'self' and lifestyle on a more everyday scale include the ready acceptance of sub-brands in the cars which we buy (a Ford Mondeo Ghia is perceived as more upmarket and therefore more desirable than a Ford Mondeo LS), the success of furniture showrooms which depict all the 'right' brands in different room settings and the surge in popularity of Nike Town, which is seen within its market segment as a lifestyle mecca.[9]

Needs versus wants

There are many lifestyle segmentation schemes available, and it's important to avoid making sweeping cultural assumptions. For example, the Stanford Research Institute has developed a number of value-based lifestyle segmentation schemes around the descriptors VALS1, VALS2 and Japan VALS for North America, Europe and Japan respectively, all of which are based on attitudes, product usage and behaviour and are useful attempts to identify patterns or segments of lifestyle and other cultural behaviour across international borders. An alternative is the *List of Values* (LOV) approach adopted by the University of Michigan, which aims to assess value fulfilment.[10] Much of

needs, wants

VALS

List of Values

the thinking behind the VALS approach comes from Abraham Maslow's hierarchy of human needs.

Maslow's 'Hierarchy of Needs' was developed in the 1950s and is now the most widely recognised humanistic theory on motivation, which it explains through an understanding of people's needs. In essence, the need to provide a safe and dry home is more urgent and pressing than the need to acquire a Ferrari, and our recognition of our own needs is a powerful motivator to meet the specific need in question before moving on to meet another but less pressing need. Maslow's theory remains valid today and is extensively used by marketers to facilitate their understanding of human motivation, management training and personal development.

Each of us is motivated by needs. Our most basic needs are inborn, having evolved over tens of thousands of years, and *Maslow's Hierarchy of Needs* (see Figure 6.1) helps to explain how these needs motivate us all.

Maslow, Hierarchy of Needs

Figure 6.1: Maslow's Hierarchy of Needs

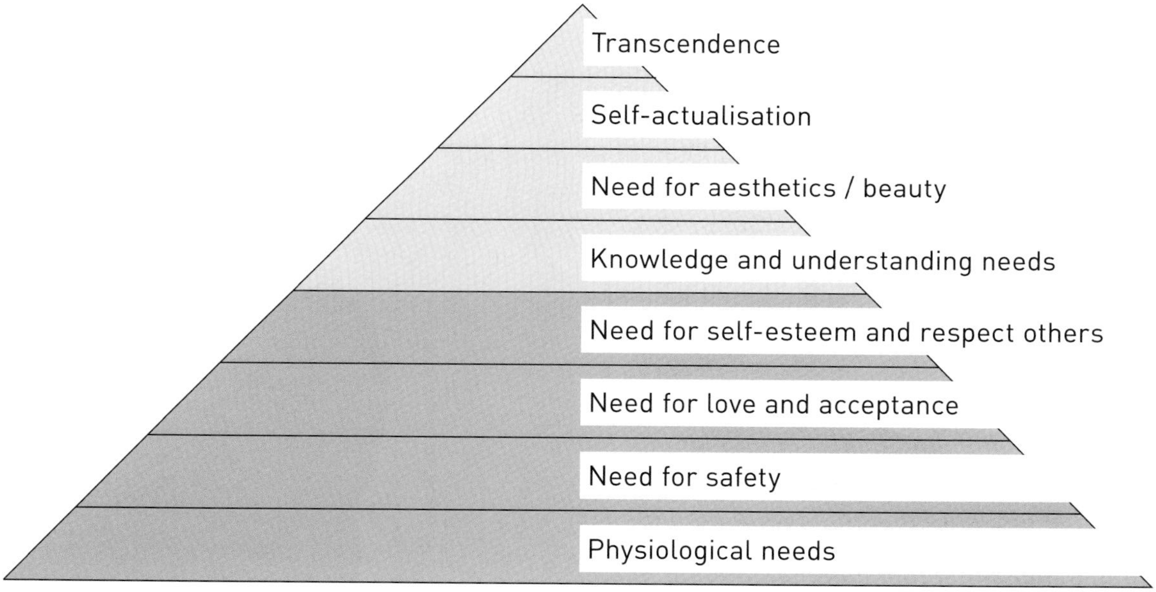

The pyramidal hierarchy recognises the following stages:
1. *Biological and physiological needs:* air, food, drink, shelter, warmth, sex, sleep, etc.
2. *Safety needs:* protection from elements, security, order, law, limits, stability, etc.
3. *Belongingness and love needs:* work group, family, affection, relationships, etc.
4. *Esteem needs:* self-esteem, achievement, mastery, independence, status, dominance, prestige, managerial responsibility, etc.
5. *Cognitive needs:* knowledge, meaning, etc.
6. *Aesthetic needs:* appreciation of and search for beauty, balance, form, etc.

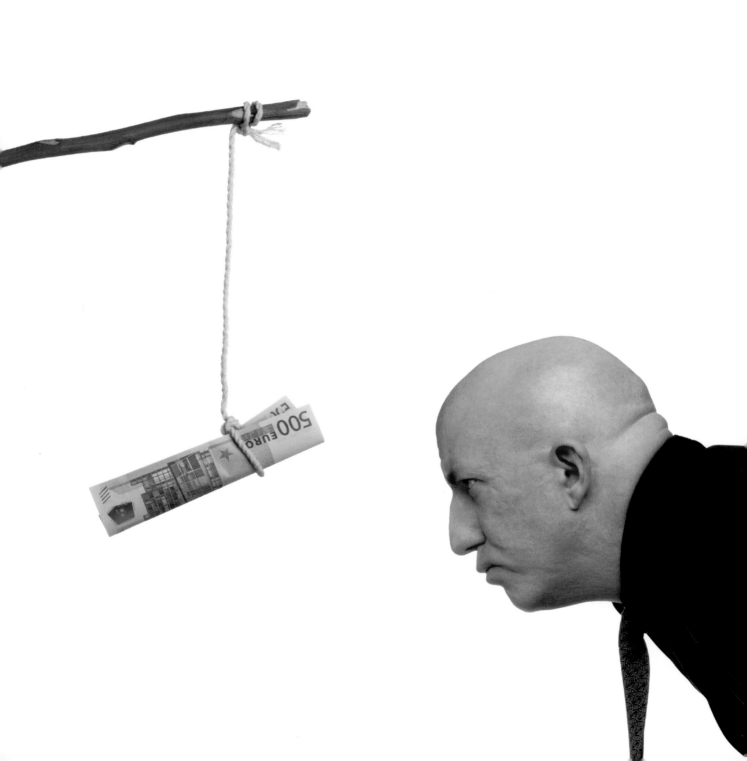

7 *Self-actualisation needs:* realising personal potential, self-fulfilment, seeking personal growth and peak experiences.

8 *Transcendence needs:* helping others to achieve self actualisation.

These needs fall into two principal categories:

- *Primary:* These are innate, often biological needs, such as the needs for food, shelter, sleep, safety and sex, and are common to all animals. They are thought to be hereditary in origin.

- *Secondary:* These are developed through interaction with other humans and are more social in origin. They might include the need to feel loved, the desire for a tactile relationship with others and the wish for friendship based on shared values rather than on a common threat or enemy. Secondary needs may also reflect status and we may share some of these needs with other primates.

'Self-actualisation' and 'Transcendence', the two categories coloured grey in Figure 6.1, were referred to by Maslow but not classed by him as either primary or secondary needs.

Maslow's theory states that we must satisfy each category of need in turn, starting with the first, which consists of the most basic needs for survival itself. Only when the lower-order needs of physical and emotional wellbeing are satisfied do we concern ourselves with the higher-order needs of influence and personal development. Conversely, if the things that satisfy our lower-order needs are swept away, we are no longer concerned about the maintenance of our higher-order needs.

motivation   *Motivation*, the response to fulfil the need, can also be broken down into several categories:

1 *Internal motivation:* a drive to achieve something of purely personal value, such as running a marathon or climbing a mountain just for the sake of it

2 *External motivation:* running the marathon to gain sponsorship for a worthy cause which the person values and supports

3 *Positive motivation:* acting in a certain way to achieve a reward

4 *Negative motivation:* acting in a certain way to avoid a punishment.

Intriguingly, while we all understand the term 'carrot and stick' as a description of the way in which modern motivational management employs both positive and negative forms of motivation, I have yet to find anyone who responds well to negative motivation. In basic terms, most of us will leave the detailed 'grunt' work of administration until the last possible moment, and many organisations have found it necessary to threaten with punishment if necessary work is not done on time; but, where bigger issues are involved, most organisations recognise the superior motivating power of the carrot to the stick.

In the marketing context, however, consumers are almost hard-wired to want the services and products which avoid or prevent an unpleasant outcome. The insurance industry, for instance, is predicated on the widespread fear of disaster. whether personal or more general, and any trip to a pharmacy will demonstrate the lengths we are prepared to go to in order to avoid the symptoms associated with a cold, a cough, indigestion, halitosis, athlete's foot – the list is endless. These products are sold to us with a clear understanding on the part of the marketers concerned that we all have a price that we are prepared to pay to avoid certain outcomes. The involvement of our

emotions in these purchasing decisions is very clear, but our motives for using, purchasing or having ready certain products and services can be divided into three distinct categories: rational, emotional and instinctive.

The motivation to purchase something is rarely based on just one of these categories, and the power of human emotion is well understood by those who wish to sell us products and services. My motivation to buy a fantastic fishing rod arises from a combination of all three categories:

1 I can construct a simple, powerful rational argument for this new rod. It will be beautifully made, will last a lifetime and comes in a very attractive, protective carrier which, rationally, I can see will be both useful and sensible. It is the pinnacle of rods in my view, so I am unlikely ever to need another rod in my lifetime and it therefore represents a sound investment.

2 Emotionally, I covet a similar rod to the one a fellow fisherman in my syndicate uses. To have such a rod would certainly make me feel good and I am, quite frankly, a trifle envious of him when I see him using the rod.

3 Instinctively, I just know that this rod and I are destined to be together, so why wait? I have no doubt that we will make an excellent partnership and I simply cannot wait to try the rod out.

If I had to explain my decision to my wife or my bank manager, I would probably major on the rational argument, because it's sensible and defensible. If I had to be honest with myself, I would admit that the rational case is just a platform that allows me to start the process in earnest and that it would be the emotional and instinctive elements of the purchasing decision which would sway me most powerfully. Research quoted by Ray *Wright*[11] shows that up to 80% of consumer products are purchased for emotional reasons, whereas rational motivation accounts for a similar level of business-to-business sales. Wright's book on consumer behaviour has an excellent section on motivation and a useful introduction to this observation about categories of motivation and motivational theory.

Wright

Wright relates the observation to what *Plato* said in *The Republic* about the divided soul. Plato argued that the soul was composed of three interrelated parts: *logos*, the reasoning part of the soul; *thumos*, the spirited part; and *epithumia*, the desiring part. Each of these parts has a separate personality and goal associated with it. Wright argues that the consumer thinks with these same three 'brains' – the rational (the head), the emotional (the heart) and the instinctive (the gut).

Plato

When we buy something, we generally use all three 'brains' in the decision making process, but some people routinely use one part more than another. Additionally, some purchases are purely impulse purchases: sweets, for example, are positioned close to the till in a petrol station so that we may notice them and impulsively purchase something we may want but don't need. Other decisions are more emotional: I may set out to buy a white shirt to wear with a suit but may choose, when I'm in the shop, to buy a blue striped shirt because I simply like it more. Other decisions again are entirely rational: if I need a tree surgeon but I don't know any, I'll go to the Yellow Pages and look for the one nearest to where I live. Similarly, if I have no loyalty to any brand of petrol, I'll choose to go to the next garage on my side of the road, in order not to have to waste time crossing the stream of

traffic. Petrol is a commodity and my decisions about fuel purchases are entirely rational.

A moment's thought tells us that rational decisions require the construction of a reasoned argument for a particular course of action and therefore involve the highest level of thought. Emotional decisions require less thought, and instinctive decisions, by their very nature, require the least thought. Whatever level of thought is required, the decisions made will be formulated on the basis of and in relation to the brand attributes and brand values of the product or service concerned.

As an example, I might choose to change my mobile phone. I don't have to worry about keeping my old number because all airtime providers in the UK now provide this service, so my first rational criterion has been taken care of. I can go to any number of retailers, but I have no particular loyalty to any of the high street shops in my town and need to find something to anchor my decision to. My favourite car magazine carries an advertisement for mobile phones from Virgin Mobile, and with that I have immediately found a starting point. I like and trust the car magazine and feel instinctively that it will be read by a number of like-minded people, so I feel comfortable with the advertisement that appears there. I like the idea of Virgin companies: I respect Richard Branson and his approach and achievements, and somehow the Virgin brand appeals to me. Its brand values are all things that I like to think I should be associated with – youthfulness, technology, today's culture, fashion – and so I feel both an affinity with and some trust in these brand values and the brand itself. I can buy a phone on line or in a Virgin megastore, which gives me total flexibility to exercise my decision with the comfort of convenience. I'll be in London later this week, so I'll go into a store when it suits me. When I go, I'll easily find someone to advise me on the best phone to buy, in a retail environment that offers massive choice. There are dummy phones to look at and handle, and plenty of technical information to help me substantiate the rational part of the decision. There is no doubt in my mind that I'll buy a phone there; all that remains is to decide which one.

In this example, I've unconsciously employed all three 'brains' in the process of making a decision. I started with an instinctive feeling of empathy with the retail brand because it was familiar and considered safe. I brought some emotional factors into the process because I like the brand values that make Virgin a 'trendy' retail outlet that reflects youthfulness and current fashion. Finally, rationally, I value the choice offered, the advice given by trained staff and the availability of technical information. In the final stage of this purchase, I'll almost certainly revert to an emotional process in choosing the phone that I feel looks best, feels nicest to use, won't make a bulge in my jacket pocket and, most important of all, will say something about me – that I am a fashionista, perhaps, or that (this being a 'business' phone) I'll look serious and competent when I use it.

Whatever the reasoning, conscious or unconscious, I will have used a modicum of rational thought to justify the purchase to myself and/or anyone else I need to involve, and a large dose of instinctive and emotional thought to enjoy the process and the end purchase. This is where consumer purchasing behaviour differs greatly from business-to-business purchasing behaviour.

As a consumer, I shall set out to ensure that this will be a satisfactory experience and, ideally, a pleasurable one. There are some gender differences here: if a woman goes shopping for a coat, she may prefer to take a friend or family member with her. This is both for company and as a fail-safe

mechanism to prevent her from making a hideous mistake. In many cases, she will see a coat she likes at the first or second shop but will trawl the entire high street before making a decision which may well be to purchase the first coat she saw. She will have refined the search by excluding shops that she knows are too cheap or too expensive, shops which have only clothes for geriatric ladies or teenagers, and shops whose carrier bags she wouldn't be seen dead carrying along the street. The *brand values* of the retailer often play a huge part in the purchasing decision. The little black dress from Chanel says so much more about you than a dress from Primark. Clearly there are differences between needs and wants. The woman might need a new dress to go to a function because her only other dress has been torn. That's a genuine need. However, she may already have several serviceable dresses but choose to buy another because she wants something new and different. In real terms, the difference between the Chanel and Primark dresses is mostly a function of want, governed by available budget, rather than need.

brand value

Men, conversely, like to settle the shopping as far as possible in one easy movement. Before embarking on the High Street, many men will have targeted a certain retailer and attempted to find something there that is adequate. Men are less likely to trawl the High Street and far more likely to go shopping alone.

Of course, these are over-simplified and stereotypical observations, particularly since men are far more fashion aware today than they were fifty years ago, but there are differences in approach and we all know and understand them innately. Consumer psyche requires us to achieve a satisfactory outcome, and we all differ in what we consider to be satisfactory. What is clear is that, should the purchasing experience be inadequate and unrewarding, either at the time or when the goods are taken home, there will be a sense of disappointment that goes further than a fleeting sensation. In the days when people bought more records than today, saving up for an album was part of every teenager's life. The process of anticipation and then carrying the prized record home to listen to was something eagerly awaited, and buying the record brought an almost tactile sense of achievement. How often, though, did we find that out of twelve tracks there were only three that we really liked? And then how frequently would we look at that album cover as if it had somehow failed us or let us down? Our sense of disappointment was clear, but we didn't like to associate the disappointment with our own shortcomings, preferring to blame some invisible record industry person who had foisted this disappointment upon us. It wasn't really our fault, and so our fragile relationship with the recording artist suffered a memorable blow. 'Once bitten, twice shy' is the proverb, and in the consumer thought process we might make that decision once, even twice, but we'd be unlikely to repeat it a third time.

Avoiding an unpleasant experience is a natural and instinctive part of human behaviour. We quickly learn that flames hurt and we are more careful in future. Similarly, we learned that records by certain bands carried too high a risk to gamble scarce pocket money on. This process is repeated day in, day out across the world, but you will never hear the sound of billions of mental cogs turning because this process is almost entirely unconscious. *Motivational conflict* occurs when we have to consider a choice that may satisfy our needs but could have a very different outcome. With the

otivational conflict

introduction of drink-driving legislation, most of us have had to consider the benefit of having just one more drink, with all the enjoyment of the drink itself and the conviviality of the moment, against the risk of being caught by the police, the loss of one's licence and, at worst, the risk of injury or even death – one's own or someone else's. This is motivational conflict on a large personal scale and most of us are able to deal with it. On a smaller scale, many of us have learned that by not buying a cream bun we can avoid the inevitable weight gain. We might really want the cream bun, but the risk of weight gain is a more powerful negative motivator.

In the 1950s, Leon *Festinger* argued that consumers couldn't comfortably manage two conflicting motivations at the same time and so would construct a strategy to deal with the problem. We are innately aware of the concept of cognitive dissonance and have devised simple strategies to avoid it. Consciously rationalising why we shouldn't purchase a cream bun is a simple construct for avoiding emotional conflict at a later stage.

Festinger

Freudian theory

Freudian theory

Sigmund Freud suggested that much of one's personality stemmed from a conflict between one's desire to gratify physical needs and one's need to be a responsible member of one's group or society. Freud, too, isolated three systems within the mind. The first is the id, which operates on the pleasure principle and seeks instant gratification and the avoidance of pain. It seems to be unaware of consequences and is self-centred and irrational. The id is counterbalanced by the superego, which functions as a conscience, building a framework of learning and experience to oppose the actions of the id. Finally, the ego tries to balance these two forces; it acts as an umpire in the battle, trying to find a way of balancing the id's need for gratification against the superego's concerns in order to find a solution that is acceptable within the environment in which we live or operate. The function of the ego is called the reality principle, for obvious reasons, and the whole process is entirely unconscious.

In the context of marketing, advertisers are sometimes able to appeal to the id in all of us by associating certain culturally undesirable aspects of their products with more acceptable symbolism. Perhaps the most commonly known example is the phallic symbolism which advertisers readily associate with cars. For many people, the car itself seems to symbolise sexual gratification, and the dismissive assertion that a man who drives a Porsche may be poorly endowed in the trousers region is familiar in common parlance. By linking a car to some phallic symbolism in this way, advertisers are able to appeal to the id in us, broaching a taboo topic that embodies a desire for sexual gratification through a clever use of association that is at once safe and suggestive.

At the unconscious level, we associate various signs and symbols with certain attributes. People trying to sell their house have learned to brew coffee or bake bread immediately prior to a viewing. We unconsciously associate the smell of coffee with the act of friendship, so the people viewing the house are being admitted into a sanctum of friendship as well as looking around the home of someone with whom they have an unconscious relationship. The smell of baking bread is symbolic of generosity, good housekeeping, warmth and welcome, so we unconsciously attribute these values by association and feel more welcome and better disposed to the vendors. We also feel that this is the kind of activity we want to associate ourselves with: we can picture ourselves baking bread and welcoming friends into that house and are thus subliminally better disposed towards purchasing it.

We all make our own associations with various foodstuffs which we find comforting. These are often based on childhood memories, if our particular childhood was a happy one. Carbohydrate-based foods are frequently cited as being redolent of comfort and security, and as I write this, digestive biscuits, macaroni cheese, ice cream and mashed potato have been suggested in a snap poll around the room. These are all different from one another but each is important to an individual. Many people in broadly similar social or economic situations may follow broadly the same consumer pattern. While we seek to find like-minded people, we also strive to overlay a degree of individuality. In the early 1980s, women of a certain socio-economic status and who dressed in a similar style were known as Sloane Rangers, the name being derived from the desirable Sloane Street at the end of Chelsea's wackier King's Road. The Sloane Ranger uniform consisted of a white shirt, a dark blue jumper and a set of pearls worn prominently around the neck. The hairstyle was made famous by Lady Diana Spencer before her marriage to Prince Charles. On the tube each morning you would see hundreds of attractive young women, all dressed in similar fashion but each adding an individual twist to the 'uniform' – an adaptation of the shirt or a variation of the cashmere jumper. Now, thirty years on, the lifestyle suggested by those who adopted this style of dress has long since passed into obscurity, but the trend has given rise to a whole new cultural marketplace for an urban style of dress.

In a recent UK TV series, wealthy entrepreneurs pretend to be poor and spend time living with people in deprived areas, with a view to finding deserving causes to support with their own money. In one episode, the man concerned is concerned that he will be identifiable by his 'city coat', and it is clear that different styles of dress are adopted by city office workers and those who do similar jobs in more rural areas. 'Power dressing' is widely recognised and understood in London, Manchester or Edinburgh but looks faintly ludicrous in Bourton on the Water. Urban consumers tend to be more materialistic and are keen to be seen in clothes with the 'right' label, to drive more aspirational cars and to have an expensive and easily identifiable, and therefore desirable, watch. Rural consumers may well be less affluent, although it is recognised that 'old money' is less flamboyant in its tastes and restraint is more acceptable.

Here, then, is another division between consumers, one that is quite apparent in the world of veterinary practice. We have seen the different approaches taken by male and female consumers and we innately recognise the differences between the needs and desires of younger and older consumers, but there would also appear to be a recognisable difference between urban and rural consumers. In a recent meeting, I spent some time talking to the principal of a group of practices based in a fashionable part of London. Not only does he have difficulty in finding young vets willing to work the extended opening hours necessary to provide a service for the commuters who form a significant element of his client base, but his clients are clearly living under considerable time pressure. When appointments run behind, his clients are far less understanding and tolerant than those in out-of-

town practices. The natural reaction to delay in the practice is now one of irritation, with some outward display of time pressure. Clients drum their fingers while waiting what he considers to be a short time to receive their bill. They also resent finding that they are not at the centre of attention if, for instance, there is a bottleneck at reception and some clients have to wait to be acknowledged while others are being served.

We are all familiar with the idea that some people are cash rich and time poor while others are cash poor and time rich. Perhaps we are seeing the emergence of differences in behaviour – whether conscious or unconscious – as the divide widens. Where else can we observe differences in real-time consumer behaviour in the real world?

REFERENCES

1 E. Arnould, L. Price and G. Zinkhan, *Consumers*, 2nd edition; McGraw-Hill, 2004

2 Ibid.

3 H.J. Eysenck and M.W. Eysenck, *Personality and individual differences: A natural science approach*; Plenum, 1985

4 R. Wright, *Consumer behaviour*; Thomson, 2006

5 G.W. Allport, *Personality: A psychological interpretation*; Henry Holt, 1937

6 http://www.thecvcoach.com/

7 N. Hellmich, in USA Today 14 February 2001 (www.bcm.edu/cnrc/annual_report/MediaActivitiesFactSheet01.pdf)

8 M. Bellis, 'Viagra, the patenting of an aphrodisiac', About.com; http://inventors.about.com/library/weekly/aa013099.htm9 A. Mitchell, 'Nine American Lifestyles: values and societal change', *The Futurist* Vol. 18 (1984), pp. 4–13

10 E. Arnould, L. Price and G. Zinkhan, *Consumers*, op. cit.

11 R. Wright, *Consumer behaviour*, op. cit.

CHAPTER VII
Self in the real world

Self in the real world

All around me are familiar faces
Worn out places, worn out faces
Bright and early for their daily races
Going nowhere, going nowhere
I find it hard to tell you
'Cos I find it hard to take
When people run in circles
It's a very, very
Mad World

Tears for Fears

VII

As we have seen, a customer is someone who will buy our goods and services, while a consumer is someone who consumes or uses them; thus, on different occasions, the pet owner will be both customer and consumer. While that might sound like a conveniently esoteric justification for stretching a concept, it really does make sense in the veterinary practice environment. The pet owner acts as a customer when making a transaction to have the dog' s claws clipped or buying poo-bags, for instance, but becomes a consumer when a more reasoned or emotional argument is required for deciding on a choice of flea treatment or life-stage food or on whether or not to proceed with an operation to amputate a damaged tail. If the pet owner is considering a commodity and no choice is being offered, once within the practice the customer has little involvement or interest in buying poo bags – they are simply an unfortunate necessity; but when something more involving and ultimately more rewarding is up for consideration, the degree of involvement forces an immediate shift to playing the role of consumer instead.

Each of us has our own tipping point, and the degree of involvement required to tip us into the consumer role will vary according to the individual. Take toilet rolls as an example. I have no brand loyalty whatsoever but have an innate preference for a certain type of toilet roll. As long as the product purchased meets these invisible and unrecorded criteria, I'm perfectly happy with whatever my wife brings home. If I'm paying the bill at the checkout, I'm just a customer of the store when it comes to the toilet rolls we purchase. My wife, on the other hand, has unconsciously identified the various possible candidates in the toilet roll aisle and will make a selection based on her preferences, by brand, by product or by reputation or recommendation – the classical filters we all use as consumers in the decision making process prior to purchasing.

So, while the pet owners using our veterinary practice may be both customers and consumers, and both at almost the same time, we have no interest in doing anything other than meeting their uninvolving commodity needs and a very real and ongoing interest in influencing their decision making process as a consumer, if we are to maintain a business relationship with that person. In the real world, the pathway is fraught with difficulties that can undermine the whole process independently of anything we do, and – quite unfairly – this does sometimes happen.

In my household, people seem to be coming and going at all times of the day and, while I'd like every mealtime to be an oasis of calm, sharing a house with teenagers and young adults seems to make that a rare occurrence. As a result, it is often impossible to calculate what shopping will be required for which days, times or people. We have found it easiest to order the bulk of the shopping on line and to have it delivered at a time convenient for the unfortunate person who drew the short straw and must be there to receive the goods. Shopping on line is intriguing. It offers none of the temptations and rewards of trawling around the supermarket, selecting luscious and promising-looking new things to try. Instead, it is a menu-led exercise, aided but not encouraged by tiny pictures of the items themselves. There is little or no temptation and scant reward to be had from trawling through linear listings and drop-down menus, so we routinely reward ourselves by including a treat – maybe a bar of chocolate or a tub of ice cream – to brighten the process and

heighten the anticipation. When the van arrives, almost without exception, something will be broken, leaking or damaged; occasionally the handles will have broken on the carrier bags containing the goods. All too often, eggs or tomatoes have been packed underneath something heavier, such as potatoes or bottles, or too much has been packed into a single bag, squashing or deforming the contents. So all that excellent attention to the retailer's brand values can easily be undone by an operational detail such as packing or transport.

During this process, I'm consciously or unconsciously assessing the quality of the service I'm receiving. Is it as I expected? Was it on time or have I been inconvenienced? Even if I had planned to stay in all day, late delivery is still irritating. Why? It really doesn't cause me a problem, as I was going to be here anyway. If goods are damaged, we'll phone the online store and, if they respond 'properly', credit us for damages and apologise, I'll be perfectly content with the process. But what to me is a 'proper' response may be an inadequate response to someone else, who might expect some form of recompense for the inconvenience.

If all is well, I remain an uninvolved customer in an unrewarding clockwork process. If something is wrong, I flip immediately into consumer mode, as I need to feel good about the decision I took, several months ago, as a consumer to use this delivery service and pay a small premium for the convenience. A poor response to my complaint may not only cause me to change suppliers but may put me off the whole online purchasing process. The online suppliers understand this perfectly and are prepared to respond more generously, more apologetically and more readily than their store-based counterparts. That's how they are trained, and the system works well – most of the time.

Intriguingly, not only might I stop buying from that particular online store if things were not handled well, but I might stop buying the branded goods involved as well. In my mind, I might associate picking and packing damage by a heavy-handed packer with inadequate or flimsy packaging that fails to protect the branded products purchased, and as a result change my buying pattern completely. As suppliers of goods and services ourselves, we can count on the fact that, just as we won't tell the online store that we've abandoned the relationship, most of our consumers would rather leave our fold quietly than stand up and make a scene.

consumption ## SELF AND *CONSUMPTION*

customer service This section might be better termed '*customer service*', as this function has now overtaken all others in consumers' ratings of establishments selling goods or services. More than the advertising spend, the marketing hype, the decor, the range of goods and services on offer, the convenience of purchasing and the sheer, naked longing and desire to buy something we really want, deep down our need to conduct a successful transaction transcends all other factors.

When pet owners are asked to rate their reasons for choosing a practice over several others, the most common reasons cited are 'service and convenience'. Convenience, however, may not mean proximity. It may mean that the practice has excellent parking, which is persuasive for this consumer, or perhaps that the practice is close to that consumer's mother, so she can drop off the children and take the dog to the vet in relative calm, even though it's six miles further from home than another practice. Unless we have a relationship which enables us to ask – and then, of course, we still have to make the effort to ask – we may never understand why our business represents convenience for consumers. On the other hand, 'service' is a concept that we all understand very well, on both sides of the fence.

Quite often, understanding 'service' and providing it don't seem to be the same thing. If we accept that the level of satisfaction with a transaction is what will affect our decision to recommend or repurchase (and both are vital to any business, unless it has a limitless ocean of new customers), then everyone involved directly or indirectly in that transaction will have played a part in determining the level of satisfaction experienced by the consumer. Initially, that level of satisfying reward will be attributed to an individual (or individuals) who have impacted positively or negatively on the experience.

Although the eponymous department which is meant to provide quality control prior to the experience and not afterwards (when it is, frankly, a tad late), 'customer service' is the dimension of the transaction experienced by the consumer at the point when that individual comes into contact with the supplier of the service itself. That moment of contact, whether brief or repeated or maintained, will have most impact on our satisfaction with the service. It will govern how we perceive the supplier and the goods or service purchased, and determine our decision whether or not to repeat the experience. Yet, although this is the part of the whole process which everyone remembers, we are really looking at it the wrong way round. The process starts far earlier on, with anticipation or preconceptions about what will happen and how satisfactory the experience may or will be. This is an unconscious assessment of our own wishlist prior to the event. It may include expectations of the degree of welcome, of enthusiasm, perhaps of recognition, assistance offered and so on, and will be subject to our own social and cultural frameworks of expected behaviour.

In today's world, most – if not all – consumers expect to be treated as the equals of whoever they are dealing with. Armed with a sheaf of downloaded diagnoses, our *Internet*-empowered consumer believes that he or she has sufficient grasp of the topic to conduct a meaningful discourse between people of equal standing. Armed, moreover, with the money to pay for the product or service, the consumer feels entitled to demand it. So, on the status checklist, our consumer is aware of no social distinction or intellectual barrier and feels financially capable of playing an equal part any discussion leading up to the transaction. Looked at from this perspective, customer expectation will be high long before embarking on the activity itself.

As we are all different, with differing backgrounds, social fabrics and cultural norms, our expectations of service will vary considerably, but the task of the supplier is to meet these invisible, undeclared expectations perfectly, time after time after time. What makes this even more difficult is that it is in our nature, particularly in British culture, to fail to comment when expectations *are* not met. and simply to drift away towards another supplier. Confusingly, we also fail to acknowledge when expectations are met. We have become so confident in our sense of self that our expectations

internet

appear entirely normal and unexceptional to us as consumers, which results in a situation where the norm of expectation is also the minimum level of delivery required. So, if one party considers their service delivery to be excellent but the recipient considers it to be merely adequate, the stage is set for misunderstanding and disappointment. This may well be compounded by body language, which, despite millions of years of evolution, remains a primeval signal box of responses to our subconscious selves. In some cultures it is demeaning to recognise service or those who provide it, while in the UK we are still not entirely comfortable with providing service and expect the full complement of recognition when we do so. Living in a multicultural world adds to the rich broth of potential problems arising from service expectations on the part of both deliverer and recipient.

So excellent service provision may be perceived by some as merely adequate. On the other hand, we have become adept at recognising poor service provision and, whatever the reality of the service provided, it is the perception of the consumer that counts. Poor service provision is likely to turn consumers away from the supplier at some stage. People's patience varies, but everyone has a limit where their elasticity is stretched to breaking point. The departure may not take place immediately, but each poor service delivery acts as a stage in the disaffection process, and it will require something which exceeds expectation to halt the slide or reverse the decline in the relationship. So, when a member of staff is interacting badly with a consumer, that might be a transient experience for the individual but it may also leave a trail of hand grenades lying in the grassy slopes of customer expectation, waiting to go off at a later stage. It always surprises me that some people believe that their occasional bouts of bad behaviour can be excused as simply 'having a bad day'. There is usually a queue of competitive businesses waiting to capitalise on other people's lack of self-control.

Measuring up to consumers' expectation of service is never easy if you can't nail what it is they may be anticipating – and, of course, some consumer's expectations will be unrealistic. How can we deal with such a collection of variables?

Let's deal first with realistic expectation. The short answer is to construct an offering which will routinely exceed normal levels of expectation, but to do this the business must start with the consumer and not with the business itself. How many times do we see businesses trying to shoehorn consumers into wanting whatever the business is able to supply, rather than finding out what consumers want and then supplying it? As an example, I recently tried to buy some hiking boots in a sale. The shop had fantastic offers on branded and desirable boots but I couldn't find any in my size. When I asked if they had my rather common size, instead of explaining that they had sold out of the most popular sizes and asking if they could perhaps interest me in something else, the sales assistant told me that the manufacturer didn't make them in my size. Crossing the road, I found the same boots in my size, but at full retail price. Needless to say, I bought them at full price from the 'honest' shop, because I felt that I'd been lied to and that made me decide never to return to the first shop ever again. For all I know, an inexperienced sales assistant might have been holding the fort, or maybe the shop owner's untrained son was filling in, but the experience was so far adrift from my expectation I felt that the shortfall was somehow disrespectful. That may seem daft, since we'd never seen each other before and probably never would again, but I took it personally at some deep

psychological level, without a nanosecond of conscious thought.

Needless to say, I didn't go back to tell him that.

We know that today's consumer has high expectations of any transactional activity and we have seen that consumers start off with the expectation that they will be treated as equals and with respect in any purchasing situation. If we go to a nice restaurant, particularly on a special occasion – nothing sharpens up expectation more than a special occasion – we will have a whole series of preconceptions even before we cross the threshold. We will have some expectations of what it will be like to sit there, what the service will be like, how good the food will be and, of course, how we will be treated by the staff. If the food is appalling, that will be disappointing and we might feel uncomfortable about having made such an error of judgement but this is a general problem that affects everyone and we can't feel singled out as individuals for this unfortunate experience. Somehow, appalling food is more acceptable than staff who are snooty and dismissive. In the latter case we will feel that we haven't been treated with respect and were certainly not perceived as equals. This is a far more personal challenge than any disappointment with the food, as it is based on human interaction and is governed by the same set of invisible and unconscious tests which we apply to all encounters with other people. The end result – a ruined evening – may be the same, but the mechanism by which we assessed the problem will be different.

In addition to needing to be treated with respect and as equals, as consumers we expect to be the centre of attention for the duration of the transaction. Imagine that you are talking to a man at a party, but that all the time you are talking to him he is looking over your shoulder to see who else has arrived. In fact, he may be concerned that his wife hasn't turned up and worried that perhaps she has met with an accident, but our first reaction will be that he doesn't find us sufficiently interesting and is hoping that someone more interesting, more important, perhaps more useful to him will turn up. We don't feel that this is an exchange of equals, we don't feel that he respects us and we certainly don't feel that we are the centre of his attention.

The same applies when we go into a shop to buy something and need the attention of a salesperson. If that person is helpful and attentive and talks only to us throughout the transaction, we will feel that the necessary conditions are in place for a successful experience. Even if we don't manage to buy the specific washing machine, for example, that we came in to buy, we will feel comfortable accepting advice and may possibly purchase something different and more expensive. If, on the other hand, the sales assistant is distracted and talks to a colleague or another customer between advising us, we are unlikely to feel that we have had the assistant's full attention or respect, or that we were the centre of his or her attention during the process. It follows that we are unlikely to buy anything from this person, let alone something more expensive than our original target.

This has obvious parallels in the veterinary practice. So often, the whole experience of taking one's pet to the vet is marred by the process of paying the bill. In the consulting room, we have – hopefully – been treated with respect, and our limited knowledge hasn't been exposed or ridiculed by the vet, so we will feel that these two pillars of consumer expectation have been met. Normally, the discussion between the vet and the owner will have been one-to-one, and there is every likelihood that the experience in the consulting room will have met our expectations and our personal series of invisible tests. When we return to the reception area, however, there are plenty of opportunities for things to go awry. The reception area will almost certainly be busy: there will be people arriving and expecting to be checked in – another battery of invisible personal tests going on there – and people telephoning to ask about opening hours, charges or directions for finding the practice, to make an appointment, to check on the progress of a hospitalised pet or for advice about vaccination. Every one of those telephone conversations may be weighted differently in importance by the reception staff, but in every case the consumer at the other end of the phone will want to be the centre of the receptionist's attention, to be treated with respect and to be considered as an equal in the process.

The person emerging from the consulting room will very often have to wait a few moments for the vet to enter the transaction on the computer and for the practice management software to show up the billable cost and whatever drug needs to be dispensed. To this day, no one has ever explained that to me, and, should the receptionist not be talking to someone else or on the phone, she will invariably be glued to the screen, waiting for the details to come up so that she can collect the fee. From the consumer's point of view, however, after having been the centre of attention just 30 seconds before, he or she now has to wait, often without apology or explanation, to be able to pay. Of course, the very nature of paid transactions requires the person with the money to feel comfortable about paying, and if I have the money I must per se be an equal in this transaction, but out there in the waiting area I'm not special or the centre of anything: my role has become functional and suddenly I'm just another client to be processed.

In veterinary practice, the most exposed position of all is that of the receptionist. Receptionists need to be masters of several trades, skilled at dealing with all the clients' requirements, welcoming clients old and new, and juggling the telephone, the cash till and the credit card machine. They also need to smile a great deal, so that everyone they deal with feels special. It's an amazingly difficult job to do well, and not every practice understands the skill sets required. Sadly, not every receptionist understands them either. The absolute bottom line is that the reception staff are the ones who conclude each transaction, whether it's a telephone enquiry or taking payment. Just as a taxing journey home after a relaxing holiday can easily spoil the whole experience, so the actions of the reception staff can make or break the whole veterinary experience. Regardless of practice policy or the carefully written SOPs (standard operating procedures) about how customer service is to be delivered, the whole experience rests on the individual at the point of contact. If this happens to be the only or the last point of contact, the consumer's assessment of the entire experience will rest on that individual.

Why, then, do most organisations – ranging from banks to airlines, from supermarkets to veterinary practices – leave the bulk of customer-facing interactions to more junior or lower-paid staff? In so many practices, the point of view of the principal or the partners is that the 'real stuff' is delivered by the vets and the need for a receptionist at all is really something of an inconvenience to the business. All the receptionist does is free the vets themselves from having to check people in and out, answer the phones and so on when they are far too busy earning the fees. The consumer's point of view is completely different. Their first contact with the practice will be with the reception staff and so, applying the same arcane set of personal but invisible tests that we all use as consumers, the process of mapping out the likelihood of a successful experience starts when we open the door and enter the reception area.

Does it smell clean? Is it welcoming? These are our first impressions, before we have even spoken to anyone. Assuming that the experience is positive so far, the next step will be to observe the body language of the receptionist. Is he open and welcoming, or do we feel that he is defending his territory with a proprietorial stance? Again, not a word has yet been spoken, but at least three invisible assessments have been made. If the practice understands the value of marketing itself professionally and realises the importance of this first and, of course, last point of contact, the whole practice experience should be under control. If, on the other hand, the practice is more concerned with cost, it may inadequately staff the business. The reception area may not be clean and fresh, the decor may not be welcoming and professional, and the staff performing this vital function may not be properly trained or may simply be the wrong people for the job.

In another life, I remember working with a practice which had noticed that its canine business was growing strongly but that the number of feline patients seemed to be dwindling. The practice was of course concerned and asked us to come in as consultants and see what was happening. It didn't take long to find out that the head receptionist hated cats. The partners had never bothered to ask and she had never mentioned it to them, but the feline clients noticed it in a flash and did what we all do in these circumstances: voted with their feet and went to another practice. Many organisations begin by shaping the business in their own image, to produce something which meets their own specifications and expectations, but think of their customers last. From the consumer's perspective, this will be instantly apparent and will inevitably be disappointing.

social factors

SOCIAL FACTORS AND SELF

Our relationship with society as a whole is amazingly complex, and many of the rules by which we live are never written down. Where does it say that the convention is for you to stand your round in the pub, that you should wear socks or that you shouldn't spit in the street? Somehow, through our upbringing and our relationships with other people, we pick up a matrix of expected behaviour as we go along. Some conventions change and some don't: men are no longer required to wear ties in many offices in the UK, but it's still not normally acceptable to wear shorts to the office. Despite these variables, our need and our ability to pick up invisible signs and pointers to acceptable behaviour remain as finely tuned as ever, and we are very receptive to a wide range of influences, whether from individuals or from groups.

Most people from the Netherlands speak extremely good English, and some thirty years ago many of them did so with a pronounced American accent (although that is less the case now). It transpires that they had learned much of the idiom of the English language from watching films and TV programmes, which came largely from the USA. So TV, radio and printed material, together

with the galactic content of the Internet, must also be seen as likely influences on consumer behaviour.

All individuals differ and are open to outside influences in different ways and to differing extents. In the veterinary context, the *Feline Advisory Bureau* (FAB) has delineated three different types of cat owner,[1] and one could easily apply the same categorisation to dog owners. FAB describes the three groups as follows:

Feline Advisory Bureau

1 dedicated

2 well intentioned

3 uneducated in cat care

The 'dedicated' client will do absolutely everything the vet suggests, immediately and with no consideration of effort, inconvenience or cost. This group represents perhaps 10% of cat owners.

The 'well intentioned' client understands the logic behind the vet's recommendations, agrees to do it all, wants to do it all and fully intends to do it, but somehow life gets in the way and the client just feels too busy. Some active stimulus is required to effect a change in behaviour but they will, eventually, get some of it done. This group probably represents around 40% of cat owners.

Finally, FAB describes the third group as 'uneducated in cat care', and this description is perhaps rather too kind, as up to 50% of UK cats rarely, if ever, see the vet for any reason at all. It is intriguing to realise that vets are largely preaching to the converted, because members of the first and second groups in FAB's study make up at least the 50% or so of the nation's pet owners who do visit the vet.

For many people, the vet is simply not the authoritative reference point that the profession should represent. Together with other professions such as doctors, lawyers and the clergy, the veterinary profession has lost the battle to be the single recognised source of relevant information in the eyes of consumers. Progressively, the professions have lost much of the respect and social standing which they enjoyed a century ago, and today's consumers are more likely to consult the Internet or ask family and friends for information than consult the vet. Perhaps they have an underlying fear that they may be charged for that information if they did so. A survey carried out by the Animal Health Trust in association with FAB made it clear that not everyone believes that the vet is the best source of information for pet health: 63% of those surveyed preferred other sources of information to the vet for advice about pets in general, and a staggering 33% chose other sources than the vet for advice about their pets' health.[2]

So, as illustrated in Figure 7.1, any two pet owners taken at random may place very different degrees of reliance on the various external sources of influence and, because these sources have hugely differing agendas, the advice and support they offer will, in turn, recommend different courses of action.

Figure 7.1: Sources of advice about pets

CONSUMER A

1 The vet
2 Internet
3 TV
4 The supermarket
5 Neighbours
6 Friends
7 Family
8 The pet store

CONSUMER B

1 The pet store
2 The supermarket
3 Family
4 Neighbours
5 Friends
6 TV
7 Internet
8 The vet

Of course, individuals and groups can influence and encourage not only socially acceptable or appropriate behaviours but also socially inappropriate or even destructive behaviours. Children's groups such as the Scouts and the Brownies require their members to embrace socially acceptable mores, such as the work ethic, kindness to others and self-sufficiency, whereas gang culture is more likely to induce destructive behaviour that is totally inappropriate for both society and individuals, by encouraging drug or alcohol abuse, violence or stealing.

Figure 7.2: Sources of influence

marketing driven source	non-market driven source	
1 Advertising Sales promotion Publicity Special events	**3** News Reviews/critique reach Programme content Clubs/organisations Cultural heroes	wide ↑ reach
2 salespeople	**4** Family Friends reach Neighbours	↓ narrow

low　　←　　　credibility　　→　　high

Key:	
Mass media delivered	**Delivered personally**

Source: W.D. Hoyer and D.J. MacInnis, Consumer behavior, 2nd edition; Houghton Mifflin, 2001 (amended)

Social influences can come from marketer- or non-marketer-dominated sources and can be delivered by the mass media or in person. Non-marketer-dominated sources tend to be the more credible of the two sets. Information delivered via the mass media has the benefit of reaching many people but may not allow for two –way communication.[3]

Additionally, there are special sources of influence. These can be individuals who are highly respected or revered as key opinion leaders, national heroes or role models; or they may be organisations acting as cultural or institutional icons, as diverse as the Church and the police.

reference groups　　　In our everyday lives, we are all to some extent influenced by *reference groups*. These are groups of people with whom individuals seek to compare themselves, as a guide to fashioning their own values, attitudes and behaviour. Marketing textbooks describe three types of reference groups:

1 aspirational
2 associative
3 dissociative.

Aspirational reference groups are those we admire and wish to emulate, but of which we are not yet

members. In Nepal, thousands of young men aspire to belong to the Gurkha regiment of the British Army. Despite a very low acceptance rate, they may train for months and even years to gain admission.

Associative reference groups are those to which we do belong. They may be small, such as a school drama club, or international, like the Masonic order. At school, other factors such as age or year group may influence membership of associative reference groups. One's gender or age may also define an associative group: activities are provided for 'Under 5s' or 'Over 60s', or one may simply join in a 'girls' night out'. Such influences may be transient – people holidaying on the same cruise liner are part of an associative group just for the duration of the cruise – or they may be long lasting. People joining the Masonic order or the Round Table tend to remain members for much of their lives.

Dissociative reference groups are those we don't want to belong to and whose ethos, attitudes or behaviour we don't want to be associated with. For instance, in the USA during the McCarthyite 1950s, being a communist would categorise you as a member of a dissociative group. From many employers' perspective, a job candidate's criminal record would suggest membership of a dissociative group of people with similar experiences. Less significantly, if a sportsman behaves badly or brings the team into disrepute, children may stop wearing shirts bearing his name for fear of such a dissociative reference.

Groups can be described as being homophilous (the Greek homophily means similarity between members) and the similarities between members may strengthen the groups influence. If the group's members think similarly and share certain beliefs, the information shared will be more credible and individuals may be more willing to accept such information at face value.

Membership of any such group doesn't necessarily indicate that an individual will follow a certain ethos or behaviour, but it is the degree of identification with that group that indicates the strength of the influence. In the 1960s, young people chose either to be Mods or Rockers. Mods were essentially modern, rode scooters, wore collarless jackets and fitted shirts, had their hair cut in a certain style and followed such bands as the Hollies and the Beatles. Rockers wore jeans and leather jackets, slicked their hair back and rode motorcycles – the bigger the better. One couldn't be both and had, to some extent, to choose between the two. The degree to which a young person adopted the code of dress became a good indicator of that person's identification with either group and with its values and standards of behaviour.

The strength of our identification with a given group may derive from either an acceptance or rejection of what our primary influencers (our parents) believed. It can also vary over time: for most of us, our parents' influence is paramount when we are very young but diminishes as we grow up. In the workplace the influence of one's school friends will be minimal, but at the age of fourteen peer pressure to conform with our associative group was breathtakingly important to us.

Socially, we are alert to other influences too. For example, we have a sensitivity to someone else's strongly held beliefs. If a person is highly religious, in many ways that will mark them out as socially different from someone who doesn't hold such strong beliefs. However if I'm told at a party

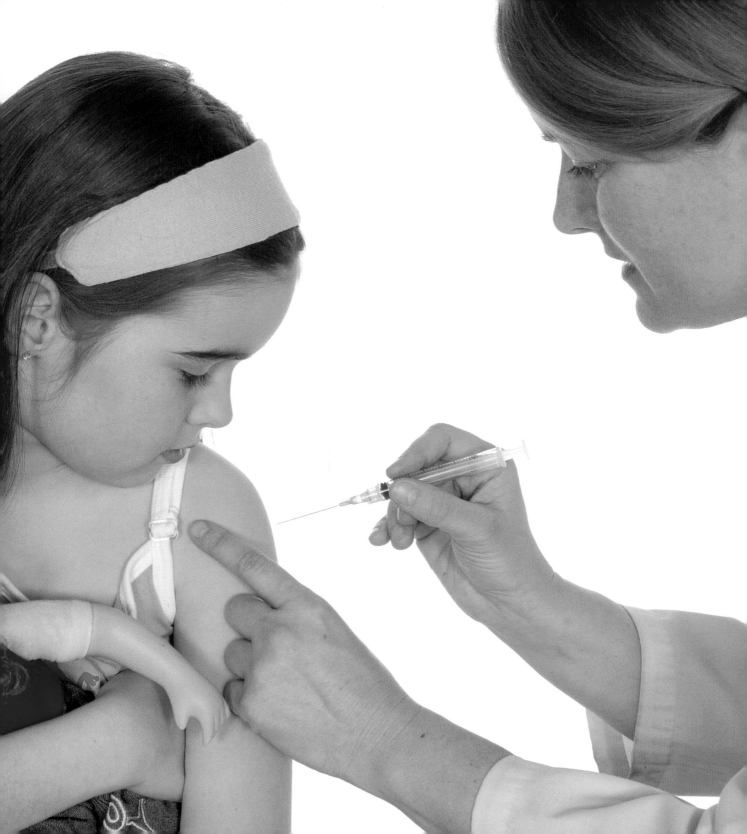

that I'm going to be introduced to Michael, who is highly religious, I've just received a coded message warning me to behave in a certain way. The unspoken instruction was that, unless I want to get into a protracted discussion about religious beliefs, it may be better to steer clear of that topic. That instruction, delivered as a hidden message, is known as a '*normative influence*' and is designed to ensure that I stay within the safe area of 'normal' discussion. It encourages conformity and reassures others in the group that social interaction will be safe and free from unsettling disturbances.

normative influence

As a society, we value norms in our behaviour and feel comforted by them, because we largely enjoy conformity. Our willingness to accept the proposition that vaccination of the majority within a certain population will control or eradicate a disease is highly influenced both by a primeval fear of disease and by our willingness to conform. If independent review and expert opinion (as seen in Figure 7.2) suggests that this is a good thing, we are generally willing to regard the argument as credible and to go along with the movement, despite a small degree of fear. But as soon as someone else credible, independent and seemingly expert raises a contradictory argument, we are left confused and largely unable to weigh up the information.

Until 1995, UK parents were happy to have their children vaccinated against measles, mumps and rubella with the single MMR vaccine. Then a study based on a comparatively small sample group was published which appeared to indicate a strong relationship between the MMR vaccine and autism in children, and over the following ten-year period vaccination levels fell from 92% to 80% and in some parts of London as low as 62%. When confronted with conflicting logical arguments, parents found themselves unable to resolve the dilemma and chose to do nothing. Intriguingly, those intelligent, lucid, articulate parents who were best equipped to accept the argument for vaccination were the ones who, within their associative groups, created a new norm of rejecting the same argument on the basis of the distant influence of a single, previously unknown researcher. Although vaccination rates are now increasing in pre-school children, it is hard to say whether this is because the link to autism has largely been disproved or because measles cases soared from only 58 cases in 1998 to 1,348 cases in 2008. 'Normative influence implies sanctions or punishments if norms are not followed and likewise implies rewards when expected behaviours are performed.'[4] The example of vaccination shows that normative influences can be long lasting, and as consumers we can adapt this reasoning to other contexts. During the late 1990s, the veterinary profession was not particularly good at reassuring pet owners about the risk of injection-site sarcoma in cats, so many cat owners turned to the Internet for advice. Much of the content posted was from the USA and a great deal of it was far from accurate, but to this day a search of the Internet will provide countless unscientific examples of pet owners' horror stories and other justifications for avoiding booster vaccinations in pets. Marketer-led data might be less credible than independent endorsement, but the public is not always adept at working out what Internet content is authoritative and what is spurious. The result is that vaccination rates remain lower than they should be, because the easiest course of action open to the confused consumer is to do nothing. What better way to justify such a wilful lack of action to oneself than to refer to unscientific Internet postings for reassurance?

The veterinary profession may not be able to control the media or Internet content, but it can

take action to put the right information into the marketplace and to encourage its dissemination through associative groups in order to re-establish a behavioural norm with positive ramifications for the daily business of veterinary practice.

REFERENCES

1	Feline Advisory Bureau Cat Group conference, Birmingham 2007
2	AHT/FAB survey 2006
3	W.D. Hoyer and D.J. MacInnis, *Consumer behavior*, 2nd edition; Houghton Mifflin, 2001
4	Ibid.

CHAPTER VIII
Influences over consumer behaviour

Influences on consumer behaviour

All the people
so many people
they all go hand in hand
hand in hand through their parklife

Know what I mean
Parklife

It's got nothing to do with vorsprung durch technic you know

Blur

DIFFERENT TYPES OF CONSUMERS

Imagine a beautiful view – you're gazing out over a fantastic landscape. Surely we're all seeing the same thing here; each person sees the same layout of hills and trees and sky ? Apparently not. According to recent research at the University of the Balearic Islands,[1] men and women respond differently to beautiful landscapes. When asked if a scene was beautiful or not, men and women both demonstrated increased electrical activity in the parietal area of the brain. In women this activation occurred both in halves of the brain, but in men the activation was restricted to the right hemisphere. Some theorise that this may be related to primeval differences when, at an early stage of human evolution, men – as hunters – needed a mental map of distance and direction while women – as gatherers – oriented themselves using landmarks to find sources of plants for food. Perhaps what we individually find beautiful has evolved from what our ancestors needed and looked for in a habitat.

So, while it may not come as too much of a surprise to those of us who try to understand the actions and reactions of our partners, it is clear that men and women think differently, respond differently in physiological terms and may well use different filters from one another in the process of decision making. Life would be complicated enough if that were the only variable, but a moment's thought reveals that there are many, many other variables. My father-in-law will soon be 80 and my younger son is 22 years old. Quite remarkably, they get on very well, and when you hear them talking they appear to have much in common. If I were didactic, I might say that they share the intolerance of others that characterises both the elderly and the still idealistic young. Either way, their thought processes seem similar enough on one plane, yet in consumer terms their approaches will be worlds apart. Their purchases will be different, their choice of retail characteristics will be different and, importantly, their points of reference will be hugely different. If both were shopping for something anodyne and ubiquitous like an electric razor, my son would respond decisively to advertisements and would already have chosen the brand before he entered the store, while my father-in-law would seek out an assistant and would want the attributes and benefits of the various products explained to him to facilitate his choice. My son would be easily sold up (persuaded to buy a more expensive version), while my father-in-law would not.

A very thrifty person might be expected to seek value in the purchase price of an item, whereas others might be more prepared to seek value in the range of attributes that a product or service offers. To most shoppers, price is not everything, and the wide variation in the offering of the main five or six supermarkets is testament to the fact that many consumers will buy a more expensive version of a product if they really believe the brand values suggesting that it will be more durable, for instance, than a cheaper version.

We have seen that there are gender differences in the way that people perceive the same opportunity. Age is a different type of filter, but it also affects people's perceptions and the way in which they undertake the buying process. When we look at that more closely, we can see that there are almost as many variations on the theme amongst older consumers as there are among more

youthful ones. What else could affect the way in which people perceive the same retail opportunity? Income and social class, family, associative groups such as friends and peers, ethnic, religious and racial subcultures are all powerful influencers of consumption and the processes involved.

different types of consumer

Of course, even within the same subcultural group, not everyone will behave in the same way. But, because there are almost 70 million people in the UK, it is simply too cumbersome to try to treat every individual separately, even though that is what, deep down, we all want from the process. Marketers have decided that it serves their purpose better to identify *different types of consumer* by the way they purchase and consume products and services. Classically, there are four types:

1 The economic and rational consumer: these are customer who make their decisions on the basis of economic rationale. These consumers will have researched the ink off the pages of various texts and endorsements in order to be capable of making 'meaningful' comparisons of all the alternative products or services available and will then make a choice based on their own evaluation. In reality, while some people purport to do this, it takes such enormous amounts of time and effort to find comparisons where all the options are expressed in similar form that very few consumers do it for themselves. While certain Internet engines will make baseline comparisons of various options for you, the devil is in the detail and very few people's requirements exactly match the criteria used by these search engines.

2 The cognitive consumer: these customers are focused on the process of purchasing, seeking to amass sufficient information to make the evaluation while accepting a certain degree of risk. Enough information will give the customer the safety blanket of having 'done the job properly' and hence reduce the risk of personal disappointment if the purchase goes wrong. In the event of catastrophe, it will be someone else's fault.

3 The emotional consumer: for these customers. information is far less important in the purchasing procedure, and they expend far less effort in amassing data. The process of purchasing is seen as an emotional reward, as the consumer's current mood and emotional state are the most powerful influences on the purchasing decision. As an example, there have been days when I have thought that stopping off on my way home to buy a book or a shirt would be a suitable salve for a difficult time at work. What women term 'retail therapy' is an entirely rational decision at the time. The following day, in the unforgiving light of reality, the rationale for the purchase might be less persuasive, but at the point of purchase the decision to buy the shirt was made to satisfy emotional needs. 'Retail therapy' is a form of chocolate for me. I don't really need the purchase but, at that moment, I want to buy something rewarding. In my case this happens once or twice a year; for millions of others it can be an everyday activity, if their emotional needs routinely drive the decision process.

4 The passive consumer: these customers are often seen as impulsive and are easily swayed by external influences, such as advertising and celebrity endorsement. Their snap judgements don't require the quantity of research that others feel impelled to perform, neither do they need to understand and evaluate a number of options side by side. Decision making in the purchasing process is rapid and probably skips several stages of rational selection.

Of course, it's far easier to be a passive consumer if one can afford to replace an item or service when it fails to deliver what is needed. Conversely, for someone with very limited financial means the process of deciding on a purchase carries more weight, because that consumer will be forced to live with the consequences of the decision far longer than a more affluent consumer would.

What about the effect of our social backgrounds and upbringing on what we purchase? In teenagers, part of the process of rebelling is to eschew the standards which our parents have imbued in us. In the late 1960s, the parents of Teddy Boys would have been appalled by the clothes their offspring wore, and that was, of course, exactly the point. A girl I know has been brought up by elderly parents who favour the colour beige. It's no huge surprise, then, that Grace favours as much bling as possible and would swoon at the chance to wear an over-the-top Moschino glittery belt with attention-getting jeans. It has taken her many years to get to this point and she's not about to stop now.

For others, however, less is more. The original appeal of Audi cars was that they were enormously understated, and it is a fundamental observation that in Northern Europe understatement is preferable to overstatement. Several years ago, many Audi drivers would, have removed all the external badging apart from the concentric rings logo. Today, things have changed: with Audi's entry-level models more modestly priced that twenty years ago, Audis have become quite aspirational cars, and some people believe that there's no point in aspiring to something if you can't broadcast your success once you have attained it.

There are clear differences between selling to individuals and business-to-business (B2B) transactions. The way a veterinary practice might do business with a single cat owner will differ from the way it would approach a local rehoming charity. The nature of B2B decision making is quite different, and further distinctions emerge in the practice's purchasing relationships, depending on whether the business is a supplier – such as a pharmaceutical company dealing directly with a practice, with a sense of pride and responsibility for the products and their research, packaging and attributes – or a wholesaler providing a route to the end user, through the practice, for a wide range of manufacturers and products, without any specific brand loyalties, or an advertising agency contracted to promote a single brand to the veterinary surgeons themselves.

All purchasing decisions are to do with resolving problems. As a consumer, suppose I need a painkiller immediately because I have a presentation to make in an hour's time and have a dreadful headache. I may employ any number of filters to my decision process, wanting to know the difference between paracetamol, ibuprofen and aspirin. I may be concerned with side effects and need to find authoritative advice. I may have difficulty in swallowing tablets and prefer capsules or a liquid or soluble product, or I may be on a train or in the car, without access to any liquid, and so need something that simply dissolves on the tongue. Alternatively, I may not care at all and will go for the first available product, trusting entirely in the packaging and the advertising hype.

Alternatively, as a manufacturer of small-animal analgesics I may want to impress on my veterinary consumers the research history, the whole process of bringing the product to market and the very individual brand attributes which I believe my individual veterinary consumer will appreciate and value. I may, however, be trying to persuade the practice to use my generic product and be attempting to make this a contractual purchase, based on price, as the analgesic of choice for the whole practice group. Both as retailers and consumers, our entire approach will differ in every individual case and there will be no written rules, no flashing lights, no easy-to-follow guide for beginners. As consumers, we understand innately what we want as individuals and what we need to do to be persuaded to purchase or consume something. Some of us will require the retailer to perform a number of functions to assist us in that process; others prefer to do the research themselves beforehand. Yet others will want to make an emotional snap decision based on their prevailing mood at the time, while others still are happier to be guided by advertising or peer pressure; for them, the need to belong to a similarly minded group may be stronger than the need to purchase an object for more rational reasons.

If we are selling, we seamlessly make that transition from wanting something to helping someone else want the same thing but, despite the fact that we are all different, in our thought processes we have to make the initial assumption that the person buying from us will see things as we do, will be guided by the same processes that we use ourselves and will seek the same form of reward from the process that we ourselves normally seek. This is one reason why vets are both reluctant to sell products and services and, in all honesty, not always very good at doing so where the consumer isn't already minded to follow their professional advice. Because vets make their decisions about which types of pet food, analgesics, anthelmintics or vaccines to recommend on the basis of research and evaluation, they tend to replay that process in full or in part to the consumer.

Of course, if we think about it for a moment we realise that not only is the consumer unlikely to have the vet's background in animal physiology and pharmacology, but their reception of what the vet is recommending will be based on what they already know and feel, whether they are young, old, time rich and cash poor or vice versa, male, female, Asian or European, rational or emotional. In addition, each client will be either more or less emotionally bonded to the pet than the client who preceded them.

An additional and rather frustrating overlay is that every minute of the day is different not only for the client but also for the vet, the nurse or the practice receptionist. Our interaction with someone else will be governed by our own emotional state, concurrent events, pressures of time or finance, or interactions within the team. The cat owner, while listening dutifully to the vet, may be thinking about whether he left the immersion heater on; and there's every chance that the vet will be wondering whether she locked the car or whether her son has actually gone to school today. This is the wallpaper of life and it applies equally to everyone of us, all the time.

As we saw in chapter 4, a great deal of what has been conveyed to the patient will be forgotten and this effect will develop over time. There are a whole raft of reasons for this. Some patients simply don't understand the terminology; some cannot actually visualise what is being explained to them, and without meaningful words to act as landmarks they don't have an adequate mechanism for retaining poorly understood data. In most of our lives we now rely on short, frequently repeated sound bites for learning new things and, despite a general loss of professional standing, doctors are

still seen by much of the population as masters of mystique. It would be a mistake to assume that all clients have the same intellectual capacity to understand and recall clinical data, but these generalisations about information recall seem to hold true in both human and animal health research.

A recent (unpublished) exercise undertaken by Onswitch Insight produced very similar results, with the fascinating insight that specific information relating to the actual diagnosis was adequately understood and recalled 7–10 days later although very little, if any, of the vet's substantive explanation could be recalled. This is why simple fact sheets can be hugely helpful in focusing attention on the key information rather than leaving it to chance that the pet owner's intellectual rigour will carry the day.

I've had a lot to remember recently. I believe I'm more or less sentient, although my children think the old boy's in danger of losing the plot and I struggle to pull people's names out of my long-term memory bank. A little while later, I can almost hear the elusive name dropping into the recall-drawer in my head, but of course by then the moment will have passed with yet another frustrating memory failure. It could down to be my age, it could be incipient Alzheimer's, or it could simply be that I'm inundated with data and that, subconsciously, I've filed some of this stuff deeper than I thought. Talking to friends about this suggests that many or even most people experience something like this once past the age of fifty. In my case it's probably down to a little of all three – or was that four?

internal customers ## INTERNAL CUSTOMERS

Marketing people quite rightly wax eloquent about brand values and the power of the practice's brand, but it's all too easy to forget that every practice has internal customers too.

The internal customers are, put simply, all the staff who have been told that Bognasty and Partners stands for customer excellence yet are invariably on hand to notice one of the partners attempting a short cut that may result in something a little short of excellence on this occasion. If a partner does it, why can't other staff do it? This way lies ruin for carefully built brand values and the practice's reputation.

The key criterion in customer service is meeting customer expectation, but all too often a practice will fail to observe and meet the internal customer's expectation of what the business stands for. Too many practices have centrally driven mission statements and notices drawing staff's attention to the five pillars of customer service, yet singularly fail to organise the staff to recognise the vision and work together to attain the customer satisfaction goals that the business espouses. These things don't just happen and they require the same investment of thought and energy as the external customer-facing activities. Customer satisfaction must not be something that some staff take seriously while others do not. In fact, total customer satisfaction can only be achieved if all customers, both internal and external, are involved and sign up fully, and where assessment of performance is seen as a necessary process rather than as a threat or a mechanism for extracting

something extra. External customers love to see a process of measurement and assessment of customer focus and will enthusiastically take part in that process if encouraged to do so. Of course, it's counterproductive to ask a consumer for his or her opinion and then promptly ignore it if it doesn't match one's own view, but businesses which actively and regularly assess their consumer-facing excellence will routinely perform better than those which don't.

The scale of some organisations is large enough for a number of employees to think themselves isolated or even insulated from client interaction: people who work in IT, for instance, or in accounts probably have little cause to come into contact with the firm's consumers. But the scale of a veterinary practice simply doesn't allow that: everyone from front desk to gardener has to be convinced by and enthusiastic to practise the ethos of a customer-facing business. This means that, even where some departments are suppliers of others, as in the case of IT, the same ethos must apply to everyone within the business.

I visited a terrific practice some months ago. The building was beautiful, there were hanging baskets outside and it looked very impressive at first sight. Inside, the reception staff were courteous and pleasant, and to all intents and purposes this appeared to be an excellent practice to bring my dogs to. The only caveat was that the parking was quite limited and, of the sixteen parking places, twelve were occupied all day, every day by staff cars. There is a double yellow line outside and, although parking is available only a hundred metres away, the staff clearly felt that the business should provide for their needs first and their consumers' second. On the wall of the staff restroom was a poster proclaiming their five tenets of customer satisfaction, yet one of the most obvious flaws in that process was apparent to everyone but the staff.

CONSUMER ATTITUDES

The whole might of consumer advertising is designed to influence and, if at all possible, change individual consumer's attitudes in favour of the subject brand or promotion. But just what is attitude and how does it affect our day-to-day lives? Broadly speaking, psychologists agree on the definition of 'attitude' as being an evaluation of an object or a concept which expresses a degree of favour or rejection. This can be an issue, a group, a person, a brand or a service. If I ask you whether you like beer, you may say that you do, and you much prefer Belgian Trappist beers to American lager-type beers and you particularly like Corsendonk beer. That's good, because so do I, but within that statement you have shown that you are *open minded*, that you are happy to *try new things*, that you have a specific attraction to strong Continental-type beers and, while you would drink a weaker, pale beer, you have a *clear preference* in your mind when the subject is aired.

You will have shown *judgement* in this process. There's no right or wrong here, but your *preference* has been expressed after a period of experiment and you have reached a *decision*. Your attitude towards beer is really an advertiser's dream because, as the highlighted words above indicate, you have demonstrated that you are open to new ideas and prepared to adapt if given a cogent reason, but can be defined within a subcategory of a product type and, therefore, reached easily.

Why do consumers have attitudes? The reason most commonly cited is that such attitudes help consumers to function within their immediate environment. It has to be an immediate environment because the attitude just discussed is only appropriate within the 'normal' environment. If I were to remove you to the Hindu Kush, where no American or Belgian beers are readily available, your attitude towards beer would no longer be relevant and would rapidly adapt to making a choice about whichever local drinks are available. Of course, these attitudes are purely internal, and unless you choose to wear a Budweiser T-shirt there will be no external signal of your attitude for others to see. We can infer your attitude by either asking questions designed to lead to a statement of your attitude or by using various stimuli associated with an attitude object. An attitude object is, clearly enough, the product, person or other item which is being evaluated.

Of course, the functions which attitudes reflect will vary from culture to culture, and in the Hindu Kush it might be more appropriate to evaluate someone's preference for yak's milk than for beer. Every individual consumer, however, will have evaluated a series of preferences, from types of breakfast cereal to whole versus skimmed milk and from types of shoes to whether or not to wear a raincoat. Many – no, *most* attitudes in our current society are founded on or affected by a series of influences, both cultural and innate, within our immediate environment. Thus most children pick up a consumer attitude towards something from their parents or siblings. Whether or not one likes a strong-tasting toothpaste is likely to be a preference developed in childhood, based on 'normal' behaviour at home. Whether or not it is cool to wear a raincoat to school is likely to be an attitude developed through the influence of one's immediate peers at a later stage of development, and whether or not one has a tendency to drink and drive will be an attitude forged within a cultural sphere influenced far more by peers and other outside forces than by parental influence.

In the context of a veterinary practice, consumers will have clearly defined attitudes towards the level of service they expect, the type and quality of decor, comfort and functionality, and the blend of all three, as well as an expectation of quality of experience. Attitudes can and do vary, usually as a result of an outside influence, and it is normal human behaviour to take an interest in anything that is different. When a new practice opens up just down the road, it is perfectly normal for people to be curious and to want to experiment. Whether or not they return to your practice may depend on multiple factors: did the new offering meet or exceed their expectations; did it provide something which they value and which their current practice fails to provide; or did it perhaps excite them and open up new possibilities?

attitude availability   Psychologists talk about '*attitude availability*' as being an evaluation of a product or service which has been stored in the memory (often acting as a benchmark) and '*attitude accessibility*' as an evaluation which is currently being experienced at a given point in time.[2] Perhaps the most important factor to know about is '*attitude strength*', which is the power to influence consumer preferences, because this is what we need in our businesses in order to attract new consumers and to regain those who have strayed.

constructed attitude   In reality, we largely arrive at decisions based on a '*constructed attitude*'; that is, one which has been pieced together from a series of different experiences. If we formulate an attitude by responding to a completely innovative experience – such as eating sushi for the first time – we may evaluate the experience and say that we quite like sushi, but, based on that single experience, our attitude will be unreliable and subject to change if and when the experience is repeated.

Most attitude objects are linked to a series of emotional experiences, feelings and thoughts which already have taken place. If a consumer has had a poor experience in a large multi-vet practice where staff turnover was high, this might result in a firmly held attitude, based on previous experience, that she doesn't like any big veterinary practices and much prefers the attention offered to her by a one-person practice. Of course, another large practice might be able to persuade her to think otherwise, but when decisions are based on previous mistakes or poor experiences these attitudes are far more difficult to influence and amend.

This is largely a reflection of cognitive dissonance: when a consumer's thoughts and expectations don't match the experience, this produces a sensation of discomfort, and the consumer then seeks some kind of action to bring expectation and experience into alignment. This could, rarely, involve giving a supplier another chance or, more frequently, lead to a further period of experimentation with one or more alternative suppliers to find the alignment sought. It is usually difficult to undo experience or unsatisfactory behaviour, so consumers will often seek to alter their expectation or beliefs in order to make that alignment easier to realise. If consumers feel that they themselves were to blame, this amendment of expectation may be more rapidly achieved, but it is likely that consumers will subconsciously seek to blame the disappointment on the supplier in general or on the individual person with whom they had the experience. This is why a second chance is so rarely an option.

Many marketers believe that each attitude is the result of three components: affect, behaviour and cognition – the *ABC of attitude*. The A for *affect* is how a consumer feels about an attitude object; the B for *behaviour* is how the consumer intends to take action, although this may not necessarily produce any action; and the C for *cognition* is how much the consumer knows – or believes to be true – about the product. All three components are important but their relative importance will depend on the consumer's degree of emotional involvement and on how engaged with or determined on the product or service the consumer is.

ABC of attitude

Of course, there is no guarantee that intention will signal action with consumers, or that intention will signal a specific, predictable action, and it is commonplace to find that consumers go out with the specific intention of carrying out a certain action – perhaps buying a rhododendron for the garden – but come back with something completely different, such as an ornamental pond. As a rough guide, we can assess a consumer's degree of conviction and reasonably expect that the higher the conviction, the greater the probability of an expected action.[3] But a mismatch between intention and action is so common that researchers now realise that life gets in the way and people's behaviour may not reflect their intentions, which is why marketers have now switched to analysing past purchases and both predicting and encouraging behaviour based on recent history rather than intention. Next time Amazon tells you on its webpage that you have bought the following books and are likely to enjoy this new title, you'll know why!

Wouldn't life be simple if every consumer action were the result of a conscious decision? Sadly for the advertising and marketing people, that's not the case. So much decision making is tied up with past experience, cultural ritual and habit, that much of what we do is apparently carried out on autopilot. How many times have you driven a stretch of motorway without any conscious recognition of landmarks or traffic patterns? When asked where we are on a certain stretch, without the benefit of obvious landmarks, we are often forced to admit to ourselves that we have been lost in reverie for the past ten miles and have little idea what has happened during that time. Culturally, this is unacceptable, and we find that admission disturbing for a whole series of reasons. Much the same pattern can occur in decision making, particularly if the decision is of low-level importance to us. Habit will have me turn left out of my drive most mornings and approach the roundabout as if I were going to Stratford on Avon, my nearest town. Only if I have a longer journey or need to catch a train will I think about turning left at the roundabout rather than going straight on. Unless I'm engaged with the process, I'm not giving it much attention.

In veterinary practice, it often happens that, after the veterinarian or nurse has patiently explained the life cycle of the flea to a consumer with a scratching dog, the staff will comment that the pet owner didn't really seem to be listening. What the consumer wants is for the dog to stop scratching now. Ideally, they would prefer the vet to give their dog an injection or pass it through some kind of chamber which would solve the problem for life – for which, of course, they would be willing to pay a significant amount of money – but permanent freedom from flea infestation isn't possible with today's technology, so, in the face of that disappointment, the next best thing is an easy and convenient remedy. A spot-on is both easy and convenient and, as long as there's no immediate health risk or danger involved, it can't be that difficult to follow the instructions on the pack. So why would the consumer engage with this process when she wants to get home and apply the spot-on before going about the rest of her day's activities, which, quite frankly, are more rewarding?

With so little engagement, there is very little need for brand comparison and little use for the A for affect, as she doesn't need to feel very engaged with the process. The C for cognition is taken care of by the vet's professional endorsement of the brand values of a respected product, so there's just room for a smattering of B for behaviour. She wants to get out of the practice and get on with her life, so she fully intends to use the product anyway. Had the conversation with the vet been about a mast cell tumour with a questionable prognosis, the engagement of A would be immediately high, C would be a priority if long-term treatment were indicated and B would be the issue as she wrestled with the factors of cost, difficulty of treatment, quality of life and so on. In this second situation, engagement would be maximal and the attention given would be far greater.

Depending on their engagement, consumers will use different models to construct their decisions. In what marketers refer to as 'prospect theory', consumers assess the likely outcome of the decision in terms of pleasure or pain, and this can also be assessed with respect to the individual

EXTRA 50% OFF
ALL SALE PRICES
WOMENS ONLY

circumstances of the owner or the animal. Hence concern for the pet's quality of life may also be tinged with some concern about whether, for instance, the owner feels that he can cope with administering insulin injections throughout the dog's lifetime.

Quite unconsciously, we make a comparison between what might be gained and what might be lost, which can be measured in terms of money, emotion, effort or commitment. The fact that losses are felt more strongly than gains may well affect our eventual decision.[4] Often we feel the need for a benchmark or reference point, which is why we like the idea of a recommended retail price. This gives us a target, either as a way of ensuring that we will not be overcharged for something or as an incentive to try to beat that price and get a bargain. Because consumers are able to assimilate a range of sources of information about product attributes, it is tempting for those who measure cognitive assessment to make the assumption that consumers will make a purchasing decision in a thoughtful and systematic fashion, but this is rarely the case. As consumers, we need to assess the attributes of the brand, which requires us to be familiar with the brand itself or to be able to list the features and attributes which our eventual decision must satisfy. This subconscious process may still be overtaken by an emotional overlay.

Rather like the way in which the British electorate often vote for the party they believe will keep out another party which they dislike, the application of a negative action in order to achieve a positive result is known as a 'non-compensatory approach'. It differs from a compensatory approach, in which a negative attribute or experience can be overcome by focusing on the positive attributes of a different brand or product. In many cases where strong brand engagement isn't present, the decision process may be one of simple elimination: less attractive brands and those with fewer listed attributes are rejected until a winner is found.

For most of us, these processes are buried deep in our subconscious and we access them, should we need to, by means of familiar mechanisms stored for just these eventualities:

Brand loyalty is a perfect tool for short-circuiting the process. 'I've always bought Ford. They've never let me down and I'm not about to change.' This makes the whole process quick and simple.

Brand familiarity is also useful. 'I need a camera. I know nothing about photography but I've got a terrific little Casio calculator. This camera looks good and it's made by Casio, so it must be good.'

'Made in Britain': For many years, the description 'Made in Britain' didn't imbue a great sense of confidence, as British manufacturing standards were not comparable to those abroad, but today it may well be enough to facilitate a decision between strawberries grown in Britain and in Ecuador.

'Special offer': Not only does everyone love a bargain, but no one wants to be considered stupid, particularly when it comes to money. The fact that something is 'cut-price', the cheapest available or good value for some other reason is often a catalyst for decision making. A local electrical warehouse sells TVs by twenty different manufacturers. If a consumer decides that he can't afford the market-leading brand, but has no knowledge of the other 'minor' brands, he may be tempted to buy on price in the absence of other obvious product attributes. This decision model may hold until he sees that one of these minor brands is made in the UK; at that point, the decision process hinges on the choice between country of origin and some other attribute. 'Special offer' and 'Made in Britain' can be a

powerful combination. Whatever the rationale or the model used, the need to avoid regret about the eventual decision will be a driving force. For many people, particularly where other decision drivers are less apparent, the strongest motivation may be to select the option they are least likely to regret, which is often the option that maintains the status quo. 'Better the devil you know' is a safe maxim to follow and avoids the need for painful introspection.

MIND GAMES WITH MONEY

Whatever currency we are familiar with, the chances are that we have a different attitude towards it from our immediate neighbour. Some people's relationship with money is entirely to do with status; for others, it is focused on acquisition and hoarding; others still have a more ephemeral relationship, with minimal interest in investment or saving. For economists money may be a simple transactional tool, but for individuals it is something with which we have a unique relationship. Why am I happy to give two pounds to someone selling *The Big Issue* in the street but incensed if someone short-changes me by that amount in a shop? Why do I feel it matters so much to be short-changed? Is it because the purchasing relationship is predicated on trust, which has been betrayed? Is it perhaps because to short-change me is an identifiable form of disrespect, and so many of our decisions are intrinsically bound up with self-esteem?

psychology of money

The *psychology of money* affects us in business, too. In a series of radio reports about how the recession was hitting a typical town, Rotherham, a newsagent from the town explained in one programme how not only the volume of his business had been affected but also the way in which people used their money. Traditionally, his business had been supported by builders and others involved in the construction industry, and they had previously paid in his shop with higher-denomination notes – £10 and £20 – saving the change in their pockets each night towards their holidays. But more recently, as the recession deepened, they had become more likely to pay for newspapers and cigarettes with small change. In their perception, the smallest significant unit of currency had changed from perhaps a £5 note to a £1 coin or even something smaller.

A recent article in the *New Scientist* suggests that people with more money tend to be happier, but only up to a point.[5] Researchers from the Universities of Illinois and Pennsylvania report that money's effect on happiness suffers from diminishing returns and, in a mirror image of Maslow's Hierarchy of Needs, once you have enough for food and shelter, more cash doesn't guarantee extra joy.[6] However, when researchers elsewhere interviewed a random sample of UK lottery winners, they found indications of significantly better mental health in large-scale winners than in non-winners or those who had won small prizes.[7]

Intriguingly, how we spend the cash is more important to us, and in a study from San Francisco State University people reported that 'experiential' purchases, such as trips to the theatre and restaurants or travel, brought significantly more pleasure than material purchases, such as clothes. While a material purchase may be more durable and last longer, a good experience brings more pleasure.

All this may seem perfectly normal and to be expected, but it appears that our attitudes to money are not entirely rational and also allow of some emotional involvement. Work from Massachusetts University suggests that modern society requires us to deal with two distinctly different rules of behaviour. On the one hand there are the 'social norms', designed to foster trust, co-operation and long-term relationships, which we see as warm and fuzzy in character, and on the other there are the 'market norms' which revolve around money and competition, encouraging consumers to put their own interests first.[8] Somehow we immediately recognise the cues or signposts for these market norms, and they trigger a form of market mentality which prompts us to think and behave in ways characteristic of these norms. As long as we keep the social and the market rules separate, everything is fine, but when the two become entwined, problems occur. Clearly, although money is regarded primarily as an inanimate tool for trade and exchange, it can easily stir up emotion and strife, so we should aim to find the right balance between these two mindsets.

It's easy to see how social and market norms can come too close together in a veterinary practice. Practitioners see their fees as a reflection of their cost structure and as both necessary and appropriate; for pet owners, on the other hand, their emotional involvement with their cat or dog is supplemented by an emotional strand in their mental treatment of money. As an example, I took both my dogs to the vet for their annual boosters and came away with flea and worm treatments as well as a treatment for atopia. I like my vet practice; I find the vets knowledgeable and perfectly pleasant, and I have no argument with what was done for my animals or with paying for the expertise and training of the vet I saw. I hadn't been thinking about the bill, but the receptionist winced apologetically as she handed me a bill for £170. I left with a sense of surprise and a fervent hope that I won't need to go back again soon. It's not that I begrudge the animals that expenditure on their behalf or that I think vets should be rewarded any less well than other professionals, but it was still a surprise and means that I have £170 less to spend on something more pleasurable. Some people may be greedy and others more needy, but we must all remember that money is a relative commodity and that everyone views it differently. That's not always easy when dealing with a fixed price list for services and products, but one thing is certain: with ten different clients, there will be ten different responses to the practice fees and ten different ways of mentally processing them.

REFERENCES

1 C.J. Cela-Condea, F.J. Ayala et al., 'Sex-related similarities and differences in the neural correlates of beauty', *Proceedings of the National Academy of Sciences of the United States of America*, DOI:10.1073, pp. 0900304106 (2009)

2 E. Arnould, L. Price and G. Zinkhan, *Consumers*, 2nd edition; McGraw-Hill, 2004

3 C. Goldsmith in *Wall Street Journal* online edition, 6 December 2004

4 J. Jacoby, C.K. Burning and T.F. Dietvorst, 'What about disposition?, *Journal of Marketing*, Vol. 41 No.2 (1977) pp. 22–28

5 M. Buchanan, 'Why money messes with your mind', *New Scientist* 21st March 2009, pp. 26–30

6 E. Diener and M. Seligman, 'Beyond money: toward an economy of well-being', *Psychological Science in the Public Interest* Vol. 5 No. 1 (2004)

7 A. Oswald and J. Gardner, 'Money And Mental Well-being: A Longitudinal Study of Medium Sized Lottery Wins', *Journal of Health Economics* Vol. 26, pp. 49–60 (2006)

8 M. Buchanan, 'Why money messes with your mind', op. cit.

CHAPTER IX
Can't get no satisfaction!

Can't get no satisfaction!

Can't get no satisfaction
When I'm drivin' in my car
And that man comes on the radio
He's tellin' me more and more
About some useless information
Supposed to fire my imagination
I can't get no, oh no no no
Hey hey hey, that's what I say

Rolling Stones

Every marketing textbook is based on the tenet that it is essential for marketing to deliver whatever is required to satisfy the consumers' needs. Even at the simplest level, however, marketers need first to understand what those needs are if they are to meet them. Modern psychologists use a variety of personality tests to measure specific behaviours and to classify consumer needs. One of them, Henry Murray, has devised a list of psychogenic needs which may, alone or in combination, lead to these 'typical' behaviours. His list of needs includes such concepts as autonomy (being independent), defendance (defending the self from attack) and play (engaging in pleasurable activities).[1]

Individuals don't accord the same value to all of these needs, and within the framework of each individual's environmental stimulus different needs are accorded a different importance according to events. Murray recognised that people willingly project their own subconscious needs onto the blank canvas of everyday life, and his Thematic Apperception Test was designed to show that, although everyone has the same basic set of needs and outside influences may affect a person's behaviour, individuals differ in their priority ranking of those needs.[2] Earlier chapters looked at the hierarchy of needs and their effect on behaviour but, the marketer will need to identify and satisfy the most pertinent need of the moment, whether it is to be in the company of like-minded people, to be in control of events and shape a planned outcome, or simply to assert one's individuality. Hence perfumers appeal to our basic needs when they promote their products: something distinctive and highly individual for the person whose need is to stand out from the crowd; something seductive and sultry if the aim is conquest; and, for those who like to be identified with the crowd, the appeal of a mass-market brand.

In the final analysis, consumers like to develop strong relationships with certain brands, particularly if they believe that a brand says something about them, but there are occasions when they look for something completely different because a new or different need is dominating their 'normal' behaviour. In today's marketplace, manufacturers seek that long-term relationship, but understanding 'their' consumers is becoming increasingly challenging as choice blossoms and individual desires are affected by multiple pressures and influences.

Whatever the particular need involved, individuals invariably base their behaviour on a need for satisfaction, although that will rarely be a conscious thought process. Why else would anyone enter into a consumption process – whether the target is food (influenced by hunger or greed), safety (influenced by fear for self or loved ones) or play (influenced by a range of emotions from boredom to hedonism) – unless the underlying desire was for a satisfactory outcome? Yet how often do we think about that when we are faced with Mrs Smith and her dog? So often, all we see is another ten-minute appointment in a day where there may be twenty or more just like it, or we reach mentally for the pharmacy cabinet while she's describing Dougal's symptoms, without taking much notice of Mrs Smith at all. After all, we may well be excited by the concept that acanthosis nigricans is a rare idiopathic genodermatitis seen exclusively in dachsunds, but for Mary Smith *(she's been married for eleven years now but still thinks of herself just as Mary, but that would be too informal a greeting, despite her need for reassurance and help. In other situations, a relationship built on friendship might develop, but most people and most practices would find that inappropriate)* the sight of Dougal scratching incessantly, with his loss

of hair and those awful great inflamed pink patches on his chest and tummy, has given her and the rest of the family sleepless nights for a week. She may be just another appointment in a busy day for the practice, but she needs and fully expects the satisfaction of 'her vet' solving the problem and magically restoring Dougal to full dermatological health.

In that moment when vet and client meet, there should be an instant accord to ensure client satisfaction, but on a huge percentage of occasions the two parties are poles apart and may never come close. The issues of formality of contact within this relationship, as mentioned above, can raise emotional no-man's-land issues with some consumers. For the consumer, satisfaction with the veterinary experience is rarely without a high emotional component, ranging from a need for reassurance and a requirement for recognition of their pride and love for a new puppy or kitten through to outright fear of the prognosis. Only rarely will their emotional state be a neutral, and this is typically when the patient is lost to the practice, as the owner drifts off the practice radar and into the clutches of the supermarket or pet store. Of course, a practice is a place of scientific achievement, often arcane in the eyes of the consumer, who has little idea of the value of a specialist qualification or the intellectual pleasure afforded to the professional by an ultrasound scanner or digital x-ray machine. Because of this, there will invariably be an element of cognition in the relationship between vet and consumer, which will have its effect on the process of expectation. It heightens the consumer's dependence on the vet, because in many cases the consumer has minimal understanding of the disease process or of the vocabulary routinely used to describe the condition, but equally it increases the gap between satisfaction and dissatisfaction, as it heightens expectancy. Clearly, service standardisation can produce a somewhat formulaic manner of dealing with consumers, which is unlikely to satisfy Mary Smith and poor, itchy Dougal.

For years, one of the profession's obsessions was that new or more aggressively competitive practices might poach or steal our clients. As we approach the end of the first decade of the new millennium, it is becoming clear to most practitioners that consumers can be fickle and promiscuous. Despite their avowed intentions, most consumers can be swayed by better service. While convenience may be a motivation, they will drive right past several practices which are demonstrably more convenient to go to the one where they believe the service level is right for them. How can we understand what is involved in delivering excellent service? Perhaps we need to start by understanding satisfaction better.

satisfaction,
dissatisfaction

SATISFACTION AND *DISSATISFACTION*: WHAT ARE THEY?

Because we cannot usually view satisfaction in the veterinary practice context without recognising the emotion–cognition combination, it is more helpful to see satisfaction as 'a judgement of a pleasurable level of consumption-related fulfilment'.[3] This immediately throws up issues to do with under-fulfilment and over-fulfilment but, because consumers will make a judgement about their degree of satisfaction on the basis of range of aspects concerned with expectation of product, brand and service levels, each of these can be seen as an opportunity to retain 'our own' consumers or attract others. Of course, it is also a golden opportunity to gift 'our own' consumers to someone else! If we give poor service but the consumer believes the values of the practice to be otherwise in line with his or her own, one poor experience will ring some alarm bells but not necessarily cause a rift in the relationship. Indeed, if excellent service is given next time, this will reinforce the consumer's feeling of satisfaction, as it will vindicate the original decision to use the practice. It may even strengthen the relationship, particularly if the practice apologises for earlier failings, but no amount of apology will make up for repeated service disappointments.

Additionally, fulfilment can mean more than the achievement of a prodromal expectation. Anticipation expects fulfilment. Nothing else will do; otherwise, we achieve disappointment. If we substitute the word 'satisfaction' for fulfilment for the purpose of this definition, a degree of satisfaction can be achieved by simply meeting expectation. Suppose that Mary Smith phones to enquire about worming Dougal. If the practice failed to note that she would be coming in, kept her waiting for ten minutes, failed to recognise who she was and then delivered a stern lecture on the need for more regular worming, that could be considered under-fulfilment.

When she comes in an hour later, as arranged, if Dougal's wormers are ready for her to collect together with a printed bill, that would meet her expectation and be adequately fulfilling. Better still, if the reception is friendly, she is recognised when she arrives, the necessary product information is imparted without giving her the feeling that she's educationally subnormal, and the whole process is fast, efficient and professional, that might well exceed her expectation and, by giving unexpected pleasure, would be an example of over-fulfilment. Similarly, if she takes Dougal to the vet because of his pruritis and the diagnosis is positive, treatment simple and prognosis cheering, the sense that things are far better than she had feared can also create a feeling of satisfaction tinged with relief that could be seen as over-fulfilment. Clearly, then, service delivery cannot be standardised to meet all expectations, although exacting practice protocols specifying high levels of friendly service offer a real safety net.

At a recent veterinary conference in Croatia, all the organiser's materials – conference bags, certificates, badges, conference notes etc. – were still impounded by customs two full weeks after their arrival in the country. Despite the innocence of the materials themselves, no amount of entreaty, bluster or bribery could effect the release of the materials in time for the start of the conference. The problem lay in the manifests, which had been completed in the wrong order, and the cultural context, which differed from what we had come to expect in the more westerly parts of Europe. There was no issue of right or wrong: it was just that our expectation was based on a 'norm' which we had developed through experience within a different culture. As the Mastercard TV advertisement says, 'there are some things which money cannot buy'. Satisfaction is both social and cultural.[4]

We should, then, be able to define dissatisfaction simply as 'an unpleasant level of consumption-related fulfilment'. While that is clearly logical, there is probably a fine line between under-fulfilment and dissatisfaction. This partly explains our national reticence about complaining and our preference to vote with our feet. If we are not particularly persuaded by the market offering of a practice that we are using, as consumers we don't need a series of major dissatisfactions to prise us away: we may well drift away because there has just been too little satisfaction.

RELATING SATISFACTION TO EXPERIENCE

A major problem for practice partners and principals is relating customer satisfaction to their marketing process and monitoring levels of such satisfaction in a competitive environment. Quite recently, a group of senior vets at a management CPD meeting were asked for a show of hands of those who routinely opened for consultations on a Sunday.

One vet called from the back, 'Jim, I didn't know that you opened on a Sunday!'

Jim replied, 'I didn't know that I was meant to tell you.'

The high level of competition between practices for a diminishing pool of pet owners willing to use the vet routinely has made imitation commonplace and consequently differentiation of products or services more difficult. Today's world demands not just that we satisfy consumer expectation, but that we build long term-relationships and develop client loyalty. Assailed by ideas such as relationship marketing and considerations such as lifetime customer value, how are practitioners to manage all this and perform their skilled work at the same time?

We know that product offerings diminish as competition increases, whereas the value of customers increases over time. In today's world, we need our customers to 'lock on' to our business and to view us as their primary choice on an ongoing basis. Customers stay with a business because they have good reason to do so, and thus 'lock-on' becomes self-iterating over time, in contrast to the transactional model, which is based on specification or price at a moment in time.[5]

Traditionally, the profession has sought to invest in attracting new customers, but that process alone will do little to reinforce product or brand satisfaction in existing customers and may lead to disgruntlement that newly attracted consumers are benefiting from introductory discounts which aren't being extended to loyal and existing customers. My son belongs to a local gym which offers first-class product attributes: excellent equipment, a spacious floor area, air conditioning, a decent relaxation and dining area and a fine pool. The fees are commensurately high, but he has chosen to pay high monthly fees to enjoy a gym which is not overcrowded, where the kit always functions properly and where there is space to relax afterwards. However, with each new membership drive his loyalty diminishes slightly. In his view, the gym is now being run for the benefit of the management and not for the members or clients. Exclusivity comes at a price which he is prepared to pay but, as membership volume increases, product benefits diminish, and I expect he will choose to look elsewhere fairly soon. If that is the case and others feel similarly, the gym's management team will need to recalculate, to see whether the loss of lifetime customer value is compensated or even exceeded by the incremental volume of business from acquiring new clients. However, as we noted earlier, consumer satisfaction is both social and cultural.

In situations where the management is aware that key customers might be preparing to leave the business, real application is required to understand the reasons why, although by this point the

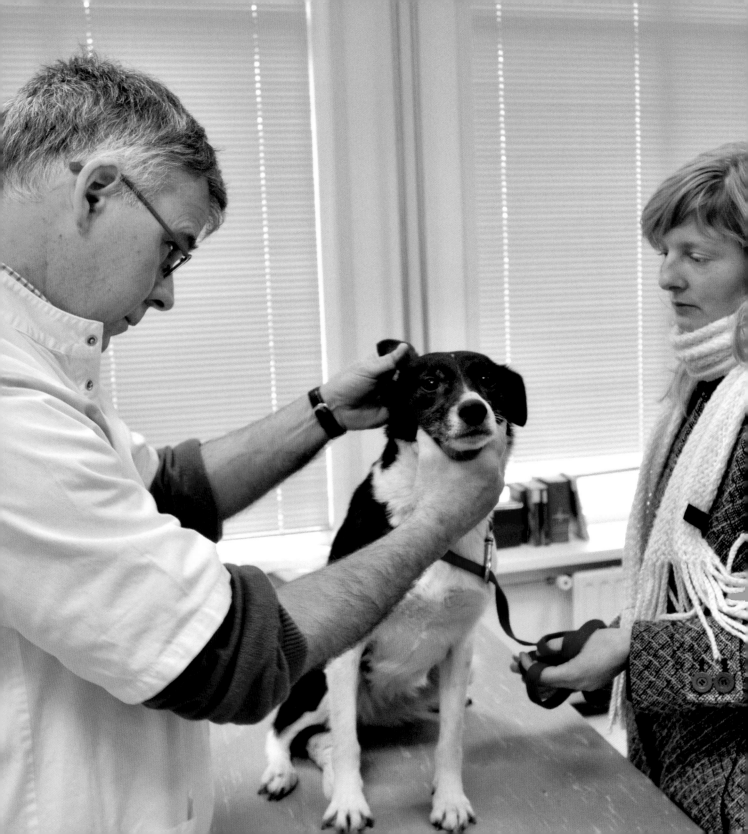

stable door is already open and the horse is, mentally, several fields away. Surely it would be far better for the business to monitor its customers' satisfaction on an ongoing basis and to be alert to any developing process of dissatisfaction. Practitioners very often ask how this can be done and laugh when it is suggested that they might appoint a client ambassador for the practice. They all too often claim that there's insufficient money to cover such an appointment, but I'd question that. If the average number of active clients is now a little fewer than 1,000 per veterinary FTE,[6] there is a pressing need to maximise client retention and to ensure that satisfaction levels are high enough for existing clients themselves to be ambassadors for the practice and thus help to attract new clients through the invaluable endorsement of friends and family. A trusted staff member with the unequivocal brief of maximising client satisfaction would cost little more than £10 per active client in a two-vet practice. Even if that person didn't actually attract any new customers, the appointment would pay its way by minimising client churn and through the incremental sale of ancillary products and services that would follow as the client cost:income ratio improved over time. New customers may help to build business, but existing customers build brand value and stabilise cash flow.[7]

Understanding how our consumers feel about us is not an optional extra in today's marketplace, and in the world of fast-moving consumer goods (FMCG) sophisticated US market-tracking services produce rankings of consumer preference. For its annual customer loyalty index, the market research firm Brand Keys surveys 16,000 consumers twice a year on their attitudes towards 158 brands in 28 categories. (Brand Keys chooses categories at its clients' request, but a brand's rank isn't affected by whether it is a client.) For each category, consumers are asked first to describe the brand attributes most important to them and then to evaluate how the brands measure up. The firm analyses the resulting data and assigns each brand a ranking in its category.[8] This information gives each brand manager the task of either maintaining the brand's high position or seeking to improve it and can easily affect the company's share price.

Reichheld   In *The Loyalty Effect*, a book which has become required reading for marketing students the world over, Frederick *Reichheld* cites several examples of lifetime customer value (LCV) in the USA, including a figure of $4,000 LCV for Domino's Pizza based on an average price of $8 per pizza. For Domino's Pizza to achieve such an LCV, one can begin to understand the value of research such as the Brand Keys data cited above. Another well used example is the data from Cadillac showing an LCV of $332,000, which indicates that a Cadillac owner typically replaces his or her car with another seven Cadillac models during the lifetime of the brand–customer relationship.[9]

To maintain this level of loyalty, Cadillac dealers kept their service bays spotless, painted the floors white and mopped the floor after each car entered or left the service bay. Cadillac customers valued this attention to detail and felt that they were being treated as a select group, membership of which was something they valued. Nothing stays the same, of course, and in the post-9/11 world and faced with a massive ecological awakening in the US car industry Cadillac may now have to find new products to appeal to its retained customers.

Perceived quality is a linchpin of customer satisfaction, and quality can be seen to incorporate both cognitive and emotional aspects of consumer judgement. In the past, a consumer would assess quality by physically handling or sampling a product, and this remains one of the cultural variables: French housewives, for example, prefer to handle fruit and vegetables before they purchase. In the Internet age, however, marketers need far more sophisticated ways of imbuing their brands with indicators of quality which can be conveyed across the ether and beamed onto a screen near you. This is clearly easier when the emotions appealed to are less visceral, and a good example can be found in the long-running campaign for Patek Philippe watches, where the message is that one never owns a Patek Philippe watch: one merely takes care of it for the next generation. This appeals to so many emotional needs – exclusivity, membership of a rarefied organisation, responsibility for a precious article, guaranteed provenance, leaving an item of real value to one's children – the list is almost endless, and each is a feel-good emotion. Whatever they paid that copywriter, it wasn't enough!

With food it's different. There's no way of conveying the spit and crackle of a frying sausage or the succulence of a ripe peach in a static screenshot, but with video so much more can be conveyed – if only the viewer can be persuaded to open the video clip. Work on food quality has majored on the basics of natural taste, full flavour, aroma and appearance, but we have ended up with supermarkets laying down categorical requirements which have produced firm, perfect-looking tomatoes with no flavour and consistently sized bananas, when what the consumer really wanted was natural-tasting, rewarding fruit and vegetables. To counter this, many supermarkets have introduced the option of local production, and my own local supermarket now makes a virtue of oddly shaped produce as being more desirable than the perfectly formed, mass-produced alternatives.

Each of us has a slightly different perception of quality, which may fit broad stereotypes but will always be highly individual. Similarly, it is almost impossible to categorise satisfaction, which remains a highly personal response. Faced with the need to book a hotel room in a strange city, what do you do? For many of us, past experience of either adequate or excellent quality may provide the key. I've been fortunate enough to travel extensively for my job over the last few decades, but hotel prices can be eye-wateringly expensive, so I now choose a budget hotel chain with which I've had adequate experiences in the past. I recognise that it may not be sited in the best location, it will not be luxurious and I shouldn't count on a high level of service, but I also know that it will offer an en-suite bathroom with clean sheets and towels and will cost a fraction of what a more upmarket chain would charge. I only expect to be in the room when I'm asleep and I can be certain of parking the car.

Satisfaction here is measured by very different criteria from those used to assess the George V Hotel in Paris. There, everything is opulent and the service impeccable, if a trifle haughty. It needs to be, because it is extremely expensive and attention to detail needs to be massively heightened for it to meet equally elevated expectations. I have low expectations of my budget hotel, but as a result it less likely to fall short of them than if my expectation had been elevated. Faced between a choice of easyJet and a traditional carrier for a short-haul route, most people would opt for the much cheaper option, but in doing so they almost consciously reduce their expectations for satisfaction. If asked whether price was the only reason for choosing the budget airline, people might falter in their response, but since enough work has been done behind the scenes to give consumers a feeling of trust in the safety, reliability and efficiency of the airline, we can make such a financial choice supported by our unconscious assessment of its quality. If the man next door, who mends his microlight in the garden shed, offered to take us up for £10, we would readily accept that price alone is an insufficient driver of our consumer decision.

choice **FEELING COMFORTABLE WITH OUR *CHOICE***

Having accepted that, where a budget hotel or airline is concerned, we will need to take on board some acceptable brand standards of real or perceived quality before we commit to a purchase, it is clear that price alone isn't enough to drive our commitment. We are well prepared to look for brand qualities and to base our purchase on an assessment of these qualities. Indeed, we are far less likely to buy an unbranded item today than we might have been twenty years ago. With branding comes a whole series of real or perceived attributes, such as safety, hygiene, ecological or social responsibility. Our own or anecdotal experience of product tampering makes it unlikely that we would buy a jar of local honey from a shabbily dressed individual on an urban street corner, but we might be charmed by the same jar of honey if sold at the roadside outside a bucolic village house by an agricultural-looking person. Perceived values are very important to us, and 'rural' suggests someone skilled in harnessing nature, whereas we suspect someone in an 'urban' environment of having a job lot of imported produce which has fallen off the back of a third-world lorry.

From a commercial point of view, a single purchase is unlikely to produce an adequate return on the capital invested in generating the sale, unless we are trading at an airport, where we are unlikely to see the same customer again. The aim is to generate regular repeat business from customers who develop a loyalty to our business, and this will be difficult if the experience is anodyne and inspires low engagement. If the experience we wish people to replicate is neither rewarding nor negative, the opportunity for customers to express their contentment or discontent may never occur. Through inertia, people will often put up with an experience which is mildly disappointing and will think nothing of it until prompted by an alternative. Many people express their wish to be content in life, but what they really hope for is happiness rather than contentment. The state of being content is actually a midline, with happiness occurring above it and unhappiness below it. Taking this on board, do we really want people to be content with our brand offering or do we instead want them to be happy with it?

Contentment and familiarity may go hand in hand, unless the experience is marginally disappointing, and then consumer theory suggests that tolerance of a mildly negative experience will result in adaptation: the response becomes modified by experience. As long as deviations from the expectation (whether positive or negative) are small, they will be accommodated and will have little effect on the reference standard.[10]

Helson Harry *Helson* proposed in 1964 that our willingness to adapt to our environment can be to our own disadvantage if habituation leads to inertia and an unwillingness to seek a better experience.[11]

If a larger deviation from expectation is experienced, however, this may change perception and lead to a change in behaviour. Furthermore, in 1991 *Westbrook* and *Oliver* showed that consumers categorise consumer satisfaction and dissatisfaction into three broad areas: negative feelings, positive feelings related to surprise and positive feelings based on interest.[12] Human nature has a need to attribute feelings and responses to some source or cause, and we are all familiar with the idea that word of mouth is a persuasive medium. Indeed, we are also familiar with the idea that worse-than-expected outcomes are more influential than better-than-expected outcomes, but why should we be surprised by that? We accept that we enter into a purchasing or consumption event with a state of aroused expectation, and so a disappointment not only challenges our level of satisfaction with the outcome but also brings into question our own judgement and the emotions related to cognitive dissonance.

Hence, with the accompanying need to attribute our emotional challenge, we should not be surprised to learn that worse-than-expected experiences are broadcast to far more people than those positive experiences which gave satisfaction. The extent of this response will depend on whether we feel that the supplier was at fault or that the problem was out of his or her control. The level of frustration may be the same, but the attribution of blame will be less if we believe that the supplier shared in our disappointment. Our willingness to accept a substitute product will also increase if we feel that the problem is shared rather than simply targeted at us.

The power of word-of-mouth comment – either positive or negative – cannot be overestimated.

Johan *Arndt* in 1967 defined word of mouth as 'product-related, oral, person-to-person communication',[13] and it takes communication onto a different plane. Instead of being a simple conveyance for information, word of mouth moves communication into the realms of transferring advice from person to person. Normally, people convey such information as if it were authoritative and impartial. when it will usually be anything but. The tonality is often that of privileged information, and this determines the relationship between the players. The person imparting this privileged information has the superior position of knowing something that the other doesn't, while the person receiving the information is made to feel special and somehow privileged. These roles are very familiar to us, because they go back to primeval times, when we had storytellers instead of TV, and are closely linked to gossip and rumour. If we doubt the power of gossip and rumour, we need only look at the plethora of magazines which exist for little reason other than convey both to a highly expectant audience.

Our willingness to believe what we are told by someone who is apparently impartial also accounts for both the appeal and the inherent danger of the Internet, where huge quantities of information exist without any cogent system for ratifying the accuracy of what we read. Yet despite this we happily turn to Google as the first step to discovering almost anything we wish to know. Our naive propensity for absolute belief in the printed word is mind boggling. Several years ago I heard Piers Morgan, then editor of the *Sun*, bravely comment that his job was to sell newspapers and not to report the news; but, despite knowing this at almost cellular level, we still yearn to believe whatever our newspaper tells us, our credulity reinforced by the fact that the newspaper we choose is a mirror to our own perceived standing in society and that, by buying that paper, we already have self-selected the tone and content of the reported news that we will receive from it.

Word of mouth is obviously a very rapid, low-effort medium for gathering information, particularly if it carries with it the inherent endorsement of a loved or respected person. Having said that, it can clearly be a more beneficial source of information if we are searching for a dentist (where word of mouth will be directly related to a painful or pain-free experience) than if we are thinking of buying a TV (where product information, established brand values and sales advice can be as powerful a source of data). Much work has been done in recent years in an attempt to ratify earlier claims that word of mouth has a massive effect on product adoption or switching, and Table 9.1 shows the power of recommendation in comparison to personal search, advertising and promotion across a number of categories. There is also the issue of comparative influence, whereby word of mouth from a trusted individual may serve to predispose a purchasing decision because advertising messages are more readily received once the recipient has been sensitised by the recommendation.[14] Thus we could suggest that word of mouth is a process designed to influence expectation.

Choice of brand provider				
	Main Source when choosing new brand/provider (%)			
Category (country)	Recommendation	Personal search	Advertising/ Promotion	Other
Coffee shop (UK)	65	20	1	14
Mobile phone airtime provider (UK)	50	24	6	20
Credit card (UK)	20	16	20	44
Car insurance (Mauritius)	60	16	6	18
Car servicing (Mauritius)	56	17	3	14
Dentist (UK)	59	3	9	30
Current car (UK)	13	42	13	33
Education institution (UK)	48	19	2	31
Mobile phone airtime provider (UK)	25	22	9	44
Optician (UK)	21	16	8	56
Bank (UK)	43	20	13	24
Mobile phone brand (UK)	21	26	16	37
House contents insurance (UK)	33	12	34	21
Car insurance (UK)	27	19	34	20
Car servicing (UK)	32	9	1	58
Dry cleaning (UK)	14	26	4	56

Choice of brand provider				
Hairdresser (Mexico)	32	29	5	34
Fashion store (Mexico)	13	27	43	17
Supermarket (Mexico)	10	36	33	21
Mobile phone airtime provider (UK)	29	13	21	37
Internet service provider (UK)	24	26	26	24
Fashion store (France)	15	47	9	29
Supermarket (France)	9	29	8	54
Means	31	22	14	32

Source: R. East, P. Gendall, K. Hammond and W. Lomax, W. 'Consumer loyalty: singular, additive or interactive?', Australasian Marketing Journal, Vol. 13 No. 2 (2005)

Table 9.1: Choice of brand provider

expectation
THE PROCESS OF *EXPECTATION*

If satisfaction is the achievement of certain anticipated standards, how do consumers measure their satisfaction? Expectation can be defined as the anticipation or prediction of future events. At its most basic level, it could be seen as a measure of hope for an expected outcome. Inevitably, consumers will anticipate that their purchase or consumption will fulfil their needs or desires, but we have seen that simply meeting expectation can be a mild negative. Such neutral confirmation of expectation may be insufficient to produce a positive feeling, which in turn will be insufficient to lead to a definite decision to repeat the process. As in most things to do with consumers, it will be the perceived effect rather than the actual effect which impacts the decision-making process, so consumers may be happy to rationalise some inconsistencies or examples of poor performance if their overall desire for a positive outcome is sufficient. The problem arises when the supplier accepts these little inconsistencies or failures as the normal operating standard, requiring the consumer in turn to compromise on this as standard behaviour. While many of us might go into an educational exam room with the idea of keeping expectation low to avoid disappointment, few of us would opt for that approach where we have both the opportunity and the free will to choose.

Consumers' expectations may be subject to cultural influence, which is often based on stereotypical information. An American friend was told that all British bathrooms are archaic by American standards and was very pleasantly surprised to find that her hotel bathroom was every bit as effective and attractive as those in the USA.

There can also be both active and passive expectations. An active expectation might be created by a body-building exerciser's claim to deliver a 10% reduction in BMI after three months' use – a dangerous claim given the variation in enthusiasm and application among its users – and a passive

expectation may be that the bottle of branded mouthwash bought in the pharmacy has not been tampered with. Additionally, some expectations may develop post-purchase. My wife simply loves the secret storage compartment in our family estate car. We didn't know it existed when we bought the car but now see it as one of the vehicle's best attributes and would actively look for something similar if we ever chose to switch brands.

Consumers' expectations don't stand still: they develop over time under the influence of a barrage of new information and product developments, together with personal experience and that of trusted partners.[15] This process is poorly understood, particularly the way in which updated expectations influence satisfaction. Intuitively, one imagines that the process is renewed each time a decision is required, but this hasn't been demonstrated.

Manufacturers understand that satisfaction is a process that persists throughout the purchasing experience and that, in some cases, it may extend to a lengthy pre-purchase fact-finding exercise. This explains why car manufacturers are eager to give journalists the opportunity to try out and write about current models: they know that, even though we may be happy with our current car, for many of us the thought process surrounding its replacement will start long before we change it. Manufacturers also understand that the need for satisfaction extends long after the purchase has taken place and usually throughout the normal life of the product. Hence a fridge that breaks down two weeks outside the warranty period will be attributed to a manufacturer building in obsolescence, whereas a calculator that performs without a fault for ten years will imbue the brand with the attributes of longevity, value and build quality.

EMOTIONS AND LOYALTY

Consumer responses to product faults may not be fair, balanced or even rational, and we also attribute distorted qualities to products which exceed our expectations. Having said that, we all have the consumer expectation that manufacturers and service providers will be fair with us, and if we perceive that a supplier has not treated us fairly the normal consumer reaction is to take our business elsewhere. Even if this proves to be inconvenient, we wish to punish the supplier (and this can often be focused on the individual concerned, as a representative of the supplying organisation). One example of this is the pet owner whose veterinary practice has chosen to use an out-of-hours service based elsewhere. The pet owner who is stressed enough to contact the practice at night or over a weekend will be expecting reassurance and familiarity with the systems and procedures of their chosen practice. If instead they have to travel to a different practice, it won't be the additional mileage which will add to their stress; it's more likely to be the need to tackle something unknown, the uncertainty of finding somewhere new, possibly in the dark, and/or the challenge of meeting new people who may not know their pet's history. When the episode is over, they won't criticise the out-of-hours practice, which did attend to their animal, but their own practice for making them go through this whole exercise. For many, this will bring their loyalty to the practice into question and increase their expectation that, when they need it most, their chosen practice will not be willing to help them. While that can be seen as a wildly emotional response, during their overnight crisis they may, at worst, have undergone a whole gamut of emotional responses, ranging from disappointment to anger and from confusion to a sense of being abandoned. At best, they may feel that their practice could have handled things better. While the partners were trying to effect a compromise which complied with the obligation to provide emergency 24/7 cover in an environment where junior staff were been unwilling to meet the stringent demands of an on-call rota, the consumers will have little or no understanding of the partners' problem and cannot be expected to be sympathetic to their plight.

Lasting customer satisfaction leads to loyalty and continued repurchasing. If a client is loyal and switching is unattractive for any number of reasons, retention of that customer should be relatively assured, until an action point of dissatisfaction is reached. We have already seen that consumer promiscuity has reached veterinary practice, with at least 20% of pet owners using more than one practice, and consumers' innate search for variety and convenience will inevitably put a strain on client retention. Conversely, in some cases the strength of the relationship may be sufficient to resist switching, and the profession put its trust in this 'bonded client' approach for many years. In reality, however, most loyal clients remain loyal because there is something in it for them. If, over time, clients become only moderately satisfied with service and performance, the practice should consider them to be bonded only at its own peril. In the end, there is no substitute for giving A1 consumer service experience on every occasion and for making the effort to monitor client enthusiasm on a personal level. If the relationship fails, many clients will attempt to understand why and will be willing to compromise their expectations of satisfaction to some extent by making attributions. However, if we accept that satisfaction has the five response modes of delight, pleasure, relief, contentment and ambivalence,[16] then both contentment and ambivalence are danger areas for any practice. Consumers always have a choice: they can stay willingly, they can wait and see, they can express their views more forcefully or they can defect to another supplier. If we define loyalty as a deep commitment to repurchase consistently, it becomes clear that this cannot be left to chance if the practice wishes to grow and prosper.

REFERENCES

1 M. Deutsch, P.T. Coleman and E. Colton Marcus, The handbook of conflict resolution; Jossey-Bass, 2006

2 M.R. Solomon, Consumer behaviour – buying, having and being, 8th edition; Pearson Education, 2009

3 R.L. Oliver, Satisfaction: a behavioral perspective on the consumer; McGraw-Hill, 1997

4 E. Arnould, L. Price and G. Zinkhan, Consumers, 2nd edition; McGraw-Hill, 2004

5 S. Crainer and D. Dearlove, Financial Times handbook of management; Prentice Hall

6 Fort Dodge Indices, March 2009

7 D.E. Schultz and H. Schultz, IMC, the next generation; McGraw-Hill 2003

8 'Taking the Measure of Customer Loyalty', Business 2.0 July 2002

9 F.F. Reichheld, The Loyalty Effect; Capstone 1996

10 R. East, M. Wright and M. Vanhuele, Consumer Behaviour; Sage 2008

11 R.A. Westbrook and R.L. Oliver, 'The dimensionality of consumption emotion patterns and consumer satisfaction', Journal of Consumer Research, Vol. 18 (1991) pp.84–91

12 Ibid.

13 J. Arndt, Johan, 'Role of Product-Related Conversations in the Diffusion of a New Product', Journal of Marketing Research, Vol. 4 No. 3 (1967) pp.291–295

14 R. East, M. Wright and M. Vanhuele, Consumer Behaviour, op. cit.

15 A. Parasuraman, L.L. Berry and V. Zeithaml, 'Understanding consumer expectations of service', Sloan Management Review Vol. 32 (spring 1991)

16 R. East, M. Wright and M. Vanhuele, Consumer Behaviour, op. cit.

CHAPTER X
All change please! Mind the gap!

All change please! Mind the gap!

Don't gimme no Buick
Son you must take my word
If there's a God up in heaven
He's got a Silver Thunderbird
You can keep your Eldorados
And the foreign car's absurd
Me I wanna go down
In a Silver Thunderbird

Marc Cohn

While no one doubts that things are changing in the mysterious world of the consumer, it would be easy to see each stage or snapshot as a cohesive situation, but this would be misleading. In reality, the changes in consumer attitudes and behaviour are always a work in progress and, while we can take soundings to see what today's snapshot shows, we should treat consumer behaviour like a sort of motorised airport walkway: its progress is inexorable and at times, however much we'd love to be able to get off, we can be carried along by it, however unwillingly.

We might think it sufficient to say simply that 'things are always changing', but as business people we need to know what is happening and we need to keep in touch with developments if we are to keep in touch with our consumers.

I have singled out three examples below to give an idea of the breadth and reach of these changes, but I readily accept that one could easily find scores of other changes to observe. These three examples have been selected because they are far reaching and will have significant knock-on effects on other behaviours; they will all, in some way, affect the manner in which we conduct veterinary practice.

adaptive behaviour **ADAPTIVE BEHAVIOUR**

Whichever way we look at it, consumer expectations are increasing and, as if that were not enough, this development is taking place at an ever-earlier age. For expectations to change, the consumer needs to be adaptive, and one of the concerns facing retailers today is the consumer's rapid assimilation of adaptive behaviour, which leads to a constantly heightened level of expectancy. Perhaps we shouldn't be too surprised by this. After all, everyone alive today has lived through (or in) a period of enormous technological change and experienced unparalleled freedom and choice. Why would they not consider this to be normal?

Much has been written about the adaptive nature of adult consumer behaviour, but less about adaptivity in children. We do know, however, that by the age of 11 or 12 children demonstrate almost adult levels of adaptivity,[1] although earlier than this their ability to adapt behaviour to changing stimuli is more limited. While there are developmental hurdles to be overcome, it is likely that in future generations adaptive behavioural skills may be exhibited by children younger than 11 or 12. What we now see as 'pester power' may well develop into something far more malleable in future. Many of us will read 'worrying' into 'malleable', but the ethics of marketing to children would fill several volumes and isn't further explored here. British children are exposed to more TV adverts than those of any other European nation, with an average of 17 adverts per hour on children's TV. Both Saatchi & Saatchi and McCann Erickson have launched children's divisions of their global advertising agencies, and advertising billboards have appeared in school playgrounds and corridors.[2] Moreover, some marketers advocate the high levels of exposure to which children are condemned as essential training for becoming discerning customers. The ITV code of conduct is extremely clear about what *pester power* is and is not be acceptable in advertising to children, and '*pester power*' is clearly banned in this code. The government's reliance on self-regulation clearly isn't working.

Fewer than half of parents think that public service broadcasting is delivering satisfactory standards, especially in reflecting a range of cultures and opinions. A 2007 report by OFCOM decried the rapidly declining contribution of commercial broadcasters to the children's TV market and found that investment in first-run programming by ITV1, GMTV and Five had halved in real terms since 1998. Specific, targeted children's media such as The Disney Channel, Nickelodeon and Cartoon Network commission some UK programming, but not nearly enough: their investment in new programmes accounts for just 10% of total UK investment. Although parents value the BBC's programming, the report highlighted the need for the BBC to strengthen its position as the largest commissioner of UK children's programming overall. ITV had dramatically scaled back its children's TV output in the preceding 12 months, in the light of both a clampdown on food advertising around children's programming and the increasing range of media available to children. The commercial broadcaster said it no longer made 'commercial sense' to include children's shows in ITV1's afternoon schedule.[3]

Nothing clarifies the picture like cash and, with the overall revenues of commercial children's broadcasters in the UK down from £178m in 2001 to £141m in 2006 (a decline of 21%) and advertising revenues down by 36% over the same period, it's clear what motivates children's TV programming. Interestingly, Sweden, Norway, Austria and Belgium all ban advertising during children's TV programmes.

Whatever the unsavoury facts, 'pester power' refers to children's ability to 'persuade' their parents or other adults to buy items or services which they don't actually need and, as children today have more influence within the family unit than ever before, advertisers know how important an influence this can be. Pester power can be divided into two categories: 'persistence' and 'importance'. The psychology is clearly different. 'Persistence' relies on constant repetition and wearing down the parent, while 'importance' appeals to the altruism of adults who presumably wish to provide the best for their offspring, and may involve the manipulation of guilt in those who feel they should spend more time or make more effort with their children.[4]

From what breakfast cereal they buy, to where the family might take its holidays, to which car would make a good family vehicle, today's children are having a dramatic impact on their families' purchasing decisions and advertisers fully understand this. Marketers plant the seeds of brand recognition in the fertile minds of children in the hope and expectation that these seeds will develop into long-term relationships. According to the Center for the American Dream, children as young as six months can form mental images of corporate logos, and recognisable brand loyalties have been established in children as young as two.[5] While fast-food and confectionery companies have been doing this for decades, we now see car manufacturers, airlines and banks adopting the same approach through children's and teen editions of magazines such as *Time*, *Sports Illustrated* and *People*, where ads are placed for adult-oriented products.

The Internet also lends itself perfectly to the promotion of products to young people. The web is part of youth culture, where children may be left exposed undisturbed and where there is no regulation. Additionally, the games market constitutes a new and hugely influential channel for marketers to reach children. The 'wannabe' lifestyle that typifies young people provides a potent vehicle for transferring adult messaging to children, and all the signs are that young people adapt more easily to new information platforms and are more aspirational than older age groups.

In every society the signals can be seen of major changes in culture, experience and affluence. One such signal, which appears to be universal in all human cultures, is the desire to travel and experience new attractions. The travel industry provides an excellent example of adaptive behaviour. Fifty years ago, travel in the UK was largely limited to the group of home nations or, if families were more adventurous, neighbouring European countries. Leisure travel was far more restricted and less adventurous, and business travel was simply embryonic compared to today's experience. Whatever their country of origin, today's travel consumers are far more aware and have access to a vast catalogue of available experience through TV and the Internet. Travel is a safe and well-loved topic for conversational transmission between friends and acquaintances, and the comparison of products and services is a necessary component of decision making over holidays and business travel.

The advent of budget airlines and ubiquitous hotel chains has encouraged tourists to eschew the packaged product in favour of creating their own holiday or business travel itinerary, and many companies will now not permit their employees to book business travel with a major scheduled airline if a budget alternative is available on the same route. The experience of others is readily available via the web and consumers are constantly looking to 'reference check' their data on line or against other trusted sources of information.

We know that the way consumers are arranging their lives, managing their free time and the interface between work and leisure, and refining their knowledge of what is available and how A compares with B or C, is changing rapidly. The lessons from this can be applied to the provision of veterinary services:

1. Consumers are taking control of how they source and absorb information.
2. Consumers are gathering information from a wide range of different sources.
3. Consumers are finding new ways to adopt more things as being 'their own'.
4. Consumers are looking for things which are genuinely different, offer better value or can be somehow personalised to their own needs.
5. Consumers are relying on trusted sites and sources of information.

Every one of these statements (which relate primarily to studies of leisure travel) has an obvious parallel in veterinary services. The questions we should be asking ourselves are:

a. What information are we offering our own consumers (and those whom we wish to impress and convert) to use for their inspiration and decision making?
b. In what ways does our product choice offer a special experience or great value?
c. How much of 'our' information is getting through?
   - How much is being filtered out because of competitive messaging?
   - How much is being drowned out by competitors?

One of the biggest changes in communication has been the comparatively recent fragmentation of messaging through new communication channels. Until the advent of Internet advertising, we had traditional methods of communication that were clearly understood by consumers. All of us were perfectly familiar with TV, radio, print (magazines and newspapers) and signage (outdoor billboards and indoor posters). Each channel was paid for by advertising or, in the case of the BBC, by levying a licence fee on the consumer.

From a marketing point of view, every advertising medium had been researched over many years, with largely predictable results and at considerable cost. The ground rules were clear and well understood by media sales companies and their clients, until the advent of digital-based advertising, which included online advertising and 'Dynamic Digital Signage' (where ads are streamed alongside other messaging on screens, whether public or private).

This market has developed significantly during the last decade, but market expectation has been confounded. Brave attempts to duplicate newspapers and journals on the web have failed, as the generation of cash from digital advertising has been slow in some sectors. Dynamic digital signage does not fall into the traditional model of advertising; many advertisers see this as a harder medium to get right and there has been significant resistance by more traditional advertisers, who prefer old-fashioned video ads on the plethora of digital TV stations to dynamic digital signage.

However, advertising companies now have not just a handful of media at their disposal, but hundreds. The options for advertising your product have fragmented from a dozen into hundreds of possibilities. It will become a requirement for advertisers to have access to expertise in each and every medium in order to maximise efficiency and return on investment, but from the consumer's point of view things have never been better. Whatever an individual's preference, there is now a series of media options tailored to meet each requirement and to appeal directly to the end user.

Together with this development has come on-demand media exposure. The advent of Internet access via mobile phone and 3G access to Internet content through other devices has transformed the ways in which people can now choose to access information and advice. Now it is 'possible for people to create and publish valuable content, for millions of Internet users to engage around passionate communities, and for thousands of websites to grow with social media features their audiences want. From small websites to multinational brands, thousands of businesses trust our products to grow their sites with the web tools, relevant content and integrated community features their audiences need.'[6]

social networking This is a quotation from the promotional webpage of a media consultancy company which specialises in providing technological solutions to communication problems by using media sources where people actively demand access rather than waiting passively for it to arrive. The whole mechanic has been catapulted into the communication stratosphere by the advent of *social networking* media such as Twitter and Facebook, to name but two. The phenomenal success of social networking, created to allow Harvard students to keep in contact with each other, could have never have been

predicted, despite the predictability of the basic human drive that fuels it. Not only has this form of social interchange altered the entire face of communication between like-minded individuals, but it has also provided an opportunity for the infinitesimally targeted media communication and promotion of products to consumers within market sectors that are more closely defined that at any time previously. The days of shotgun scatter advertising are clearly over and we now need to understand how to identify and target likely consumers actively, rather than wait hopefully for them to walk past our promotional message.

In 2005, Arbitron Inc. conducted a study into demand media and US consumers which showed that an estimated 27 million Americans owned one or more on-demand media devices – such as a DVR, iPod or other portable MP3 player – and also demonstrated a heavy tendency towards an on-demand media lifestyle.[7] The study focused on devices and services that allow Americans to exercise more control over the media they consume. Its findings were:

- Twenty-seven percent of 12- to 17-year-olds owned an iPod or other portable MP3 player.
- An estimated 43 million Americans chose to record TV programming to watch at a different time (using such technology as a VCR or TiVo DVR).
- Seventy-six percent of consumers owned at least one DVD. Thirty-nine percent had 20 or more DVDs in their personal collection.
- Awareness of XM Satellite Radio had tripled since 2002, from 17% to 50&, while awareness of Sirius Satellite Radio had increased even more significantly, from 8% to 54%.

'The study shows that consumers, while still using traditional media, have great enthusiasm and passion for on-demand media,' said Bill Rose, Senior Vice-president of Marketing, US Media Services, Arbitron Inc. 'Traditional and Internet broadcasters need to adjust their approaches to accommodate this increasingly important consumer segment.'[8]

Now, almost five years later, the spread of Sky+ media and similar devices, together with 3G telephony, Blackberry phones, hand-held and in-car navigation aids and the now ubiquitous broadband Internet access, have made demand-led access a routine activity in the UK, which no one considers surprising or unusual. Consumers are adapting just as fast as the technology that is leading them to demand new products and services.

Consumer behaviour reacts quickly to outside stimuli, and the economic downturn which has affected society almost everywhere in the world has had an effect which marketers regard as one of the most powerful reactions in marketing experience.

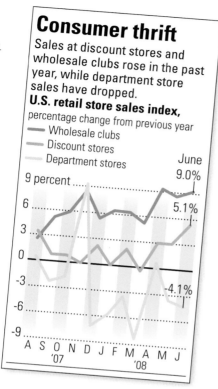

Figure 10.1

Consumer thrift

Sales at discount stores and wholesale clubs rose in the past year, while department store sales have dropped.
U.S. retail store sales index, percentage change from previous year

— Wholesale clubs
— Discount stores
— Department stores

9 percent

June
9.0%

6   5.1%

3

0

-3   -4.1%

-6

-9

A S O N D J F M A M J
'07   '08

Source: International Council of Shopping Centers, Associated Press

Concerns about prices, the unavailability of credit and insecurity of individuals' job tenure have significantly affected people's willingness to shop differently. Market research shows that there has been a fundamental shift in retailing, with previously more affluent shoppers taking to purchasing at discount stores as well as, rather than instead of, the more upmarket stores they previously supported (see Figure 10.1). Not only have they changed some of their chosen stores, but they are also buying less expensive brands. In a survey of 50,000 consumers, 63% of US shoppers had started to cut spending and, most importantly, had decided that when things recovered they would retain this more modest approach. When the economy rebounds, we can expect to see some reversion to previous habits, but what US PR company Porter Novelli describes as *'depression mentality'* suggests that this frugality may linger after the event.[9]

    For decades, it has been rumoured that it is enough just to open the doors of a decent practice for the work to come flooding in. Colleagues in large-animal practice have learned quickly that this is not the case in their speciality and have adapted to working in a different pattern and with slightly different objectives. It seems that the time is rapidly approaching when small-animal practitioners

depression mentality

will need to look at their working practices and ask themselves whether now is a good time to revise some aspects of what they do and how they do it. Without doubt, changes in consumer expectation are opening up new avenues of exploration at the same time as making some of the products and services which vets have traditionally offered look less attractive.

The advent of budget vets (a generic term rather than a reference to any specific practice) providing either limited services or a full service at a reduced margin has opened up market segmentation, and awareness of different market offerings has also gained momentum with the rapid development of corporate practices. However, as the next example shows, some consumers are struggling to find the right relationship with healthcare providers. In some larger practices consumers may not see the same vet twice, and while consumers may very much enjoy some of the benefits offered by a large small-animal practice, I believe that they still want and expect the personal relationship to continue. Clearly, those larger or corporate practices which can offer both types of benefit will be well placed to succeed with that segment of today's changing consumer base.

citizen consumers ## CITIZEN CONSUMERS

We are so used to consumers seeking special treatment from chosen retailers that this behaviour has ceased to be noteworthy and we treat it as normal. However, new research shows that people now expect to be treated as consumers by public services too, and this has become a major theme of public service reform. It is clearly not a straightforward issue, and people in different cultures perceive their relationship with public service providers differently.

Many years ago, I made my living as a medical representative selling pharmaceuticals to GPs in the morning and to pharmacies in the afternoon. In those simpler times, I covered a territory which embraced the formerly industrialised valleys of South Wales. When I first started, I was surprised to see how few people were waiting to be seen in the GPs' waiting rooms and wondered if that might be a sign of extreme efficiency or excellent standards of public health. One GP was quick to point out that, while many of the patients now lived on state benefits, most felt that they had already paid enough in tax for the NHS to offer them home visits rather than require them to come to the surgery. In their view at that time, their relationship with health care officials was one whereby the NHS was bound to provide whichever services they, the consumers, chose.

In more recent market research surveys, many people contrasted their ongoing and personal relationship with healthcare providers with the anonymity of normal consumer relationships, and for their part service providers found the concept of consumerism uncomfortable. However, the use of such terms as 'patients' and 'clients' was also found to be uncomfortable as public reactions and expectations developed. The consumers of those healthcare services believed that they had a particular, fairly intimate relationship with the healthcare providers. People regarded themselves as having multiple relationships with different service providers – they saw themselves variously as users, carers, taxpayers and citizens.

With other service providers, such as the police, the relationship differed according to the nature of their exposure to that service and was affected by the fact that, as in more familiar consumer territory, there might not be a choice of services available if the environment was deprived of resources. As tensions grow between needs, choices, rights and the resources necessary to meet these expectations, the managers of public services are finding themselves struggling to understand what the users of those services expect and, as a result, to predict service requirements accurately. Additionally, many users of these services have become far more assertive towards the institutions and organisations which are responsible for them, but more understanding and tolerant of the people who work within them. As a 2008 study of shopping habits says: 'The current policy agenda conceals the tensions between needs, choices, rights and rationing and devolves them to service organisations. Choice appears to be making those decisions more difficult. More transparency about such tensions and how they are being managed would create more productive public dialogue.'[10]

Using public services is not like shopping but, as with shopping, people want skilled, reliable people and services which they can trust. Their growing assertiveness is a signal that public expectation of any product or service for which they are required to pay is as critical in the public sector as it is in the private sector.[11]

People want services which deliver promise, but this breaks down when service providers concentrate on managing demand rather than meeting need and when the newly empowered voice of user groups transcends the stance of authority adopted by the management of some service providers.[12] As in so many other ways, consumers are adapting to change and creating the template for service providers to meet.

How this will affect the relationship between veterinary practitioners and their consumers is, as yet, unclear. The very fact that Onswitch Research has shown that around 20% of pet owners who do use the vet are using more than one practice, and that 11% of what we fondly refer to as 'bonded clients' are also using more than one practice, tells us that consumers' perceived needs are complex and difficult to anticipate. The profession would be naive to think otherwise.

What is clear is that consumers will continue to want a particular relationship with their vets which meets their urgent needs when something goes wrong. That relationship will be based on absolute trust and total confidence that their chosen vet can walk on water. Such a deep relationship may not be needed when just another supply of wormers or flea treatments is required and may not be seen as appropriate when it comes to seeking advice about their pets. Additionally, practices repeatedly put that depth of relationship at risk if they refer their out-of-hours work to other practices. If the relationship becomes damaged, we should ask ourselves which factors consumers will use in their decision where to buy their veterinary services in future. They may or may not choose to change practice, but they may well decide not to buy their elective purchases from their vet or even through the veterinary channel at all. Worse still, they may choose not to buy some services which their animals actually need but which can only be bought at the vet. The worst possible outcome for the profession would be a gradual *disengagement* from the responsibilities of pet ownership and, eventually, a disengagement from pet ownership altogether.

disengagement

As in all things, service and convenience are the watchwords of consumerland. If any of our loved ones needs something urgently, every one of us would be willing to drive miles in the wee small hours, but, human nature being what it is, we may be less tolerant and willing to put ourselves out when there's no urgency and another, easier solution can be found. These observations apply to veterinary practice too. What we may be seeing here is the beginning of a fragmentation of the market brought about not by the practices themselves in the way they promote themselves, but by the consumers who have consciously or unconsciously structured their response to the wide range of services offered within the context of their own busy lives. While it is vital for veterinary practices not to let themselves be seen as a mere commodity in the marketplace, it is simply a question of time before some practices react to such consumer-oriented positioning and promote themselves in a fashion which meets this market expectation.

There would be not a word of complaint from pet-owning consumers if this were to happen. but it may not be quite what the veterinary profession had thought would lie ahead.

REFERENCES

1 D.R. John and J. Gregan-Paxton, *The emergence of adaptive decision making in children*, *Journal of Consumer Research* 1997 pp.43–56

2 G. Monbiot, June 2009 (www. monbiot.com/archives)

3 OFCOM consultation 'Television advertising of food and drink products to children' 2006–07 (www.ofcom.org.uk/consult/condocs/foodads)

4 A. Sutherland and B. Thompson, Kidfluence: *The Marketer's Guide to Understanding and Reaching Generation Y – Kids, Tweens and Teens*; McGraw-Hill Ryerson 2001

5 'How marketers target kids' Media Awareness Network, 2009 (http://www.media-awareness.ca/english/parents/marketing/marketers_target_kids.cfm)

6 www.demandmedia.com

7 *Internet and Multimedia 2005: The On-Demand Media Consumer*

8 'Consumers changing the way they access media', *Audioholics* online audio-visual magazine 2005

9 E. Vidler and J. Clarke, 'Creating Citizen-Consumers: New Labour and the Remaking of Public Services', *Public Policy and Administration* Vol. 20 No. 2 (2005) pp. 19-37

10 'Gloomy economy changing shoppers' habits', Associated Press 20 July 2008

11 J. Clarke, *Citizen-consumers? the public and public services*; Open University 2007 (http://www.consume.bbk.ac.uk/researchfindings/citizenconsumers.pdf)

12 E. Vidler and J. Clarke, 'Creating Citizen-Consumers: New Labour and the Remaking of Public Services', op. cit.

CHAPTER XI
Global consumerism

Global consumerism

Over the mountain
Down in the valley

I've seen them all and man
They're all the same

Well, it's not just me
And it's not just you
This is all around the world

Paul Simon

THE POWER OF *THE INDIVIDUAL*

Imagine a world governed by economic heft rather than by military might. In their book *The Sovereign Individual*, James Davidson and William Rees-Mogg[1] make a cogent case for the developing power of the individual brought about by rapid changes in the factors that, throughout our previous history, had shaped world power. Subtitled 'The coming economic revolution and how to survive and prosper in it', the book looks in some detail at the mounting and nationally unaffordable cost of maintaining a meaningful military presence, as well as at the growing power of the word.

Modern technological weapons are puissant beyond our imagination, so much so that responsible nations' leaders are afraid to unleash them. National powers, dependent on their vast armoury of satellites, aircraft carriers, strike jets, tanks and rockets, are fantastic at sabre rattling, but recent conflicts have shown that, despite the technology, targeted deployment which avoids innocent civilians is at best difficult and at worst unachievable. Moreover, a few kilos of Semtex packed in a terrorist's briefcase can do untold damage to the heartland of a nation's governors, turning political opinion in ways that our elected rulers cannot manage or manipulate. On a larger scale, 9/11 has demonstrated that conventional warmongering is simply not a match for determined terrorism. The world has undergone a huge seismic geopolitical shift.

Alongside this, the original expectation that the latent power of the computer would make superstates more powerful has been proved wrong. Massive computing power is now available not only in laptop format, but at lower and lower prices. The individual has at his or her disposal access to all the world's reference books, to every detail of global history and current affairs, and to information about how to grow and cook food and make weapons of mass destruction. In this Age of Information, computer networks are the basis of all communication and are clearly changing the structure of world society. Not only is an individual able to bring a government to its knees through terrorism, but that same individual can hide his or her money in any of the world's banks, speculate in any economy and avoid the very taxation needed by governments to fund their military presence.

Superstates such as the USA, the former Soviet Union, China and the developing and ever-widening European Union have been built on a favourable balance between the massive power of the state and the relative weakness of the individual. Since finance is the basis of nation states, we should expect economic terrorism, either through malicious design or hapless greed and lax controls, to pose an ever-present threat to our national security and wellbeing, particularly as individuals discover the power to use communication technology for such purposes. Writing in 1988, Davidson and Rees-Mogg foretold the collapse of the superstate, leaving a fragmented China and European Union and a shrinking Russia. In part, they were correct. The Soviet Union collapsed in 1991 and, while the European Union has been hugely enlarged, it is clear that a two-level membership structure will be necessary if smaller countries are to remain members and Franco-German control is to be retained. Already, calls for a European joint military force have been dismissed and several countries have, by referendum, rejected membership of the single currency. Additionally, the population of Western Europe is shrinking. Italy was the first European nation to

declare a net shrinkage of its population, but the situation is more extreme in Russia: by 2030 Russia's population will be 18 million smaller than it was in 2008 and by 2050 it will be 50 million smaller than in 2008. By that date, Italy's population will have shrunk by 20 million.

new consumers ## THE *NEW CONSUMERS*

It's hard for us in Western Europe, with our history of development propelled by a largely Catholic church and with our domination of that history through exploration and colonialism, warfare and art, culture and faith, to get our heads around the scale of the impending changes in socio-demographics. However, by 2015 the three most wealthy territories in the world will be Taiwan, Singapore and Hong Kong. With a population of 5 million and a GDP of US$80 billion, their per capita wealth will exceed that of any other nation. Moreover, an explosion in the middle-class populations of India and China will produce a vast multitude of new global consumers. China's middle class will number 290 million by 2011 and 520 million by 2025. By that date, India will have over 500 million new middle-class consumers.[2]

Staying with this shift in demographics for a moment, the next 40 years will see China, India, Brazil, Russia, Mexico and Indonesia becoming six of the world's seven biggest economies. Despite its shrinking population, Russia will remain massively powerful in economic terms because, together with Brazil, it will dominate the world's resources, while Indochina will dominate manufacturing. Nigeria, Turkey and Vietnam are also expected to come within the world's top 15 nations for economic size, and most of these nations, unlike the UK, have comparatively youthful populations. The UK, on the other hand, has a comparatively ageing population with the over-90s as the fastest-growing age group.

If we assume that the world has historically been shaped by younger societies, many of the formerly dominant societies, largely those of Western Europe, are now ageing and have shackled themselves with high standards of living dependent on complex incomes derived from alternatives to shrinking manufacturing and agricultural industries. This leaves them less able to compete with today's young, vibrant, exploding populations of middle-class consumers hungry to catch up with the West's higher per-capita income and spending. It's a sobering thought that half the world's population in 2008 had never made a telephone call. If we just think what changes to infrastructure will be needed to cater for this exploding demand, it becomes easier to see how Europe will increasingly decline as an economic force until the ageing population/economy cycle creeps around to these newer economies too. In comparison with Europe, the USA has a relatively young economy and we can expect it to continue to grow as we decline.

As European populations shrink, we shall lose skills and competitive edge. We have already lost much of our manufacturing capacity to the East and have seen a shift from growing and rearing our own food in high-cost Western Europe towards a growing dependency on crops and livestock in Eastern Europe, where growing and rearing costs are far lower. Instead, we have drifted towards the specialised processing of premium products for niche and luxury markets, bringing about a clamour to protect 'titles of origin' for such products as Parmesan and Camembert cheeses, Parma ham and Scotch whisky.

Another global change has been the shift from rural to urban living. 2007 marked the first year when more people lived in towns and cities, and we should expect to see mega-cities of 25 million and more in Shanghai, Sao Paulo and elsewhere. In Britain, however, the population growth in rural areas has actually outstripped that in urban areas for each of the last four decades.[3]

The effects of these world changes will be felt everywhere, in various ways. The demand for food will not only multiply dramatically, but as new populations become more affluent their demand to ascend the protein chain in their choice of foodstuffs will increase. The provision of education and healthcare are other areas where we shall see soaring demand. For example, if the demand for healthcare in the USA continues to grow at its current rate, by 2026 the US demand for trained nurses will exceed the current total output of trained nurses worldwide.[4]

GLOBAL BRANDS

global brands

These trends will bring masses of new global brands, in much the same way as we have seen a gradual and gentle assimilation of Japanese and Korean brands into our economy over the last twenty years. While we wait for these brands, commodities have already gone global. Even in 2003, the EU was buying more than half of Russia's oil and 62% of its gas exports. Contracts for gas were already commonly denominated in euros, and a fifth of the natural gas consumed in the EU was Russian. It is also easy to see why both parties to an oil contract might benefit from billing and payment in euros. Europe is Russia's natural trading partner and the euro zone now extends to the Russian border, with the addition of Poland, Slovakia and Hungary. The EU wants Russia to recycle its petro-euros, buying capital goods from European manufacturers and removing for both sides the risk of reliance on the dollar.[5]

So major change in the supply of commodities and resources will have negotiated or forced effects on the value of major currencies, affecting the economies and lifestyles of people the world over. 'So what?', you might say: 'We're affluent now and all these things are relative.'

The real point of trying to gauge the future is not simply to foresee how life will be in 2050, a time which many of us are unlikely to see, but to anticipate what will happen tomorrow. As Bellini said, 'These changes will not suddenly happen on July 12th 2049, we are in the future, it is happening now.'[6]

In 2005, with amazing prescience, Shell International published its global scenarios for the following twenty years. One section focused on '*Low Trust Globalisation*',[7] in which the world sees mounting pressure for global-scale regulation but ends up responding to it with a patchwork of often conflicting rules. 'Regulatory Competition', however painful, is proposed in order to achieve a balance between respect for market forces and efficient intervention by state regulation. All these predictions have come true, long before 2025. The global financial collapse which started with sub-prime mortgages in the USA was an accident just waiting to happen, since individual and corporate

Low Trust
Globalisation

greed were not just allowed to flourish but were exhorted as appropriate behaviour by a system which had long since lost its way and where the regulators acted in only a nominal fashion.

In the veterinary area, the harmonisation of UK and European legislation, designed to uphold the values enshrined in the EU's stance on competition, actively removed any semblance of a monopoly on the sale of certain therapeutic products for cats and dogs and created an unholy alliance with any manufacturer willing to play. By this means, products intended by the licensing system for veterinary sale only were made available not just within the newly and specially created SQP tier but also as GSL products, without restriction or the requirement for advice to be given. Consumers and the veterinary profession, who had hitherto seen drug licensing as a measure of efficacy, potency and risk, now found themselves regarding the UK licensing system as a mechanism to facilitate the uptake of certain active agents for the good of the overall pet population. If spot-on flea treatments, safe for dogs but known to be lethal to cats when used accidentally, are given preferential treatment in the market because the government takes the view that it's worth losing some cats to ensure that more dogs are controlled cheaply and effectively, then consumers should want to know that this manipulation has taken place, on their behalf but without their permission. If an active agent in one flea treatment is considered worthy of a POM (prescription-only medicine) licence and therefore distributed exclusively through vets and pharmacies and only available on prescription, while an otherwise identical product is made available through any outlet, without prescription or advice being required, this risks destroying consumer trust in the licensing system.

What of the veterinary future in the globalised world? We should expect patterns of pet ownership to change in the UK. With an increasingly selfish younger generation and an increasingly active senior generation, there may be pressure either to do without pets altogether or to select low-maintenance pets such as small furries or ornamental fish. On the other hand, a burgeoning population of silver surfers may, as a result of their increased Internet usage, be far better-informed and more enthusiastic pet owners than they were before. There is no doubt that our urban sprawls are expanding in the UK, and we have also seen significant immigration. For many of these people, the UK is a place to visit for several months or years but with the aim of returning home. They may send money home during their stay in the UK and are more likely to rent than to own property. Current financial pressures will be off-putting for new pet owners, and most practices have reported an increase in the number of price-checking phone calls received from people who are sounding out practices for the value of their services and, incidentally, ascertaining the true costs of keeping a pet.

The globalisation of brand awareness, of financial expectation, of music and film, the instantaneous nature of the Internet, the availability of new book and film releases simultaneously throughout the world – all these factors precondition our consumers. When asked who might be the most famous person in the world, living or dead, one answer was David Beckham. No other sportsman, possibly no other recognisable figure, could command such global awareness as David Beckham and one can imagine that even Mongolian households might be aware of his existence, even if they knew little or nothing about him. The TV and the Internet have acted as cultural

gatekeepers on a vast scale, filtering and funnelling any information that has value to an organisation or movement which seeks to influence behaviour. In many cases, we can see consumer-generated content, and we also see market research blossoming in the least sexy places – in airports, on buses and in shops – as companies pay attention to people's wants and needs in shaping future products. Social networking contributes a rich seam of consumer input and helps to form 'like-minded' people's opinions.

We have seen a migration of emphasis from top-down to bottom-up in the way persuasion is marketed; when my wife jokingly tells her friends that, to get me to do something, she has to make it look as if it were my idea, this is exactly what manufacturers do every day to create demand. Michael Solomon[8] talks about living in 'consumerspace', where customers act as partners with manufacturers to help companies decide what the marketplace should offer. He cites the example of Microsoft beta-testing market-ready software: many of the 650,000 customers who bought the software were prepared to pay Microsoft a fee to be part of the testing programme, because it would teach them how to use the package more effectively and more lucratively within their businesses.

Whatever happens to our UK pet population, we can expect the more adventurous manufacturers to find a way of sending DTC (direct to consumer) messages to pet owners, bypassing the vet's communication channel but relying on the vet, as one of a series of gatekeepers, for distribution of the product. It won't be long before a pharmaceutical company has a TV advert showing puppies eating snails and cautioning against angiostrongylus, or showing a dog walking by a canal and warning that regular vaccination against leptospirosis in dogs is still necessary.

Similarly, we should expect to find consumers forming alliances with major pharmaceutical or nutritional manufacturers, completely independently of their veterinary surgeons. As mergers and acquisitions continue, we may see a market dominated by three mega-companies, with perhaps one hundred smaller niche manufacturers running alongside. We shall see considerable growth in generic formulations of drugs, partly because of the same costs which forced the mergers and acquisitions in the first place, and we should expect to see far more consumer-led government intervention in packaging and labelling, as well as in the provision of novel delivery systems for animal as well as human drugs. Because of globalisation, we can see financial possibilities for the distribution of products on a far wider scale; already, most veterinary nutritional products carry four to six languages on the packaging and many drugs boast pack inserts in multiple languages. As this trend develops, more and more companies are developing relationships to achieve customer-led innovation, which encourages engineers and designers to 'dream' with customers.[9]

This already exists in the electrical and home sectors. Today photocopiers, tomorrow novel vaccines in novel delivery systems, delivered to your door by a veterinarian who manages your pet's health and is different from the veterinarian who mends the sick and broken pet. Why not? If it can be made to work in Manhattan it will be made to work in Morley and in Mexico.

INFORMATION WE CAN TRUST?

The instantaneous nature of news transmission works equally effectively for consumer news as it does for world events, and in some cases the crossover is plain. When Michael Jackson died, the second news wave, following the immediate discovery of his death, focused on the world's loss of a star entertainer. Within hours, the Internet was full of special compilations, video offers and other memorabilia. The line between what is right or wrong, respectful or inappropriate, has been irretrievably blurred by the interests of those who stand to benefit financially. Similarly, when the Scottish Parliament chose to release Al-Megrahi, the only person convicted of the 1988 bombing of Pan Am Flight 103, which exploded over the town of Lockerbie in Scotland, the world's media fell into a feeding frenzy.

The Scottish government released Al-Megrahi on compassionate grounds and allowed him to return to Libya; across the globe, TV coverage beamed out pictures of Libya's rapturous welcome party, in which jubilant spectators waved Scottish saltire flags to the horror of millions in the UK and the USA, where most of the Flight 103 passengers had originated. A week later, a poll suggested that the majority of Scots believed their government's decision to release Al-Megrahi was wrong. Only 32% of the 1,005 people questioned by ICM Research said they agreed with the Scottish government's decision to free Al-Megrahi on compassionate grounds, while 60% of respondents said it was the wrong thing to do, according to the survey by the BBC. Almost 70% of respondents said they believed that factors other than legal grounds had influenced the decision by Scottish justice secretary Kenny MacAskill.[10]

Whatever the rights or wrongs, whatever the arrangements conducted behind the scenes – and most of us believe that some discourse must have taken place between the governments of the countries involved – the news coverage leaves the reader or viewer with the inconclusive but persuasive impression that the decision was incompetent. In the fashioning of public opinion, the news media has never been in such a powerful position, with the ability to reach into people's lives 24/7 and through a myriad of channels in which we have willingly personalised our receptiveness, whether that be via TV, radio, email, newspaper or online coverage streamed through our laptops, desktops and mobile phones.

In much the same way as we choose to provide mobile advertising for 'fashionable' brands by displaying their logos on our clothing and personal goods, we have blurred the line between the objective provision of news and a subjective commentary on events through our active engagement with an elective relationship with news providers. News provision is accompanied by a constant stream of promotional advertising, yet we confidently predict that our behaviour will not be swayed by this content. The success of the media agencies who sell these opportunities to reach out to all of us is testament to our failure to manage this interface. At the same time, this blurring of the edges is important to the news providers, as it allows them to escape the need to complete their investigations or confirm their sources. In a situation where constant news provision is a requirement to power the media machine, anything else would be unaffordable in both time and resources.

From the perspective of the consumer, however, the more the edges become blurred, the more accepting consumers become of incomplete data. The process is hardly new and has been developing for half a century, but has now reached its zenith with our obsession with celebrity. Countless newspapers, magazines and TV programmes cater for this apparently international desire to know more about people whom we 'meet' through their reputation for music, sport or entertainment. These media discuss the individuals, their social and private lives, their clothing, appearance and finances, but at no stage will they offer a balanced picture. As a result, millions of people believe what has been written and make their value judgements accordingly,. Whether it be the release of a convicted Libyan bomber or the private life of a minor TV personality, people are increasingly content to believe whatever they read, see or hear, with no real requirement for a balanced or accurate picture. Whether they live in Melbourne, Macclesfield or Montana, they will be able to access the same information and reach the same conclusions simultaneously.

We malign people if we assume that they have no interest in whether what they read is true, but we have gradually come to accept a lower degree of veracity in the supply of information. Wikipedia is probably the leading provider of vast swathes of online information, but it relies on its readers to maintain standards of accuracy. While this solution might not cause me much loss of sleep if I were enquiring about the age of David Beckham, I might feel the need for a more reliable source of information if I wanted to assemble a home-made bomb. As a mere consumer, I genuinely don't know how to rate or grade the content of various sites and so have alighted on a simple solution, rather similar to my choice of newspaper. I have chosen one newspaper to read, having more or less satisfied myself that it takes a responsible stance, and have solved my 'problem' on line by selecting a favourite information source which I assume to be fairly reliable. Of course, I have no idea what influences – social, political, religious or otherwise – will be brought to bear on this new generation of data providers. but I'll probably fudge it just as I have with my newspaper.

All over the world, consumers are seeking brands with which they can identify. Whether these brands are financial, FMCG, pharmaceutical, sporting or connectivity-driven, we all want to feel that we have sought out brands which best represent our own feelings and emotions. I have a soft spot for the Co-operative Bank because I have a sense that it has demonstrated some ecological responsibility, which is important to me. In reality, I've cheerfully swallowed a part of a story which, although I have made no effort to research it properly, appears to fit with my image of myself and my own values. At the same time, I quite like the idea of supporting local businesses and will actively choose locally produced food if I can.

I have a mortgage with Abbey, who are now owned by the Spanish conglomerate Santander. Mentally, I'm still with Abbey, even though I know that this is now nothing more than a brand. I know nothing about Santander, because I've never taken the trouble to find out, but, because it's now in the UK and associated with my trusted brand Abbey, I'm prepared to believe that it's one of the good guys. Yet had the adviser suggested going to a major Spanish financial house for a quote when I took out the mortgage, I imagine I would have been reluctant to do so. Why? I would probably have thought that it would be a brand unknown to me and, therefore, outside my comfort zone. In fact, Santander's performance throughout the recent credit crunch has been exemplary in comparison to other 'trusted' brands in the UK, which only proves that my flawed decision process has been built on the shifting sands of prejudice fuelled by absolute ignorance. Am I very different from the other 61 million people in the UK? Somehow I doubt it.

So, if Santander has become a respected and trusted brand in such a short period of time, will we want to extend our trust to other international brands too? Of course! Look at KLM, the Dutch national airline, Microsoft, the US giant software company, Perrier, the producer of bottled water (which we all assume to be French, like the brand itself), Danish Bacon, Zurich insurance, Kerrygold butter and Sony electronics, to name just a few. All these are brands that we've grown up with and which, as a result, we somehow perceive to be local because of our familiarity with them. While the French still enjoy a largely protectionist economy and actively choose French produce, the British consumer has readily accepted brands from all around the world for several decades. Will we so willingly accept new brands from Brazil, Russia, India and China (the BRIC countries) as their populations and economies blossom in the next two decades? This grouping of countries will soon come to dominate world economies but is as yet largely unknown on the sophisticated stage of consumer opinion. What will make them acceptable is the alchemy of the advertising and marketing industries which will portray these brands as having something which we believe we crave, and if they are successful we shall come to trust these brands and their inherent brand values too.

The world is changing, of course, and, while we may favour the gentle social responsibility stance of the Co-op, we have also to face up to the growing dilemmas raised by GM foods, the need for biofuels to replace other edible crops in limited farming space and a raft of other, more challenging bio-considerations. To date, the public has chosen to hide behind its ignorance and largely ignore the existence of GM products. In so doing, it has eschewed the responsibility of making a decision. Where it's a matter of a simple choice between foodstuffs, such as breakfast cereals, where we can make an 'informed' decision, it's easy for us to move forward. Where, however, it's a matter of the billions more mouths that will need feeding in emergent nations over the next two decades, consumer opinion will need to be massaged into believing that any ethical or other social or moral implications should be overridden by the pragmatic necessity of driving food production to a new but still affordable level.

Consumer acceptance is fickle and hard to predict but, in true Maslow style, it is based on a desire to avoid missing out on something, provided we have enough of the basics to be able to concentrate precious time and resources on seeking such gratification. As billions of new middle-class consumers come into the BRIC marketplace, there will be an explosion of brands designed to satisfy them. How many of these new brands will come to the West too? How we accept them will depend on how they are portrayed to us by advertisers, but in reality we will have little in common with the brand values of manufacturers in Russia, India or China and will naively be placing our trust in conglomerates which we fail to understand. Whether or not they will be constructed with the same social and moral responsibility that we require in the currently affluent Western world still remains to be seen, and one can easily imagine that many of these emergent brands, while entirely

announced that

quisition yesterday

product offerings in hum

small molecules and nutri

icines in numerous growing the

manufacturing capabilities

de advancing capabilities and a lea

ned company will have some of the best asse

industry," said Jeffrey B. Kindler, chairman and c

e have a clear responsibility to turn those strengths in

customers and the communities we serve, as well as for

We will measure our success through our company's new com

de advancing wellness, prevention, treatments and cures that

health needs, while maximizing our financial perform

ed to welcome our talented new colleagues fro

scientists and business leaders," Mr. Kin

ng colleagues possess all of the hi

ject of our business, and sha

tage of life."

and Headline

global in their reach, may have to be produced with different priorities in mind.

When things go wrong, as they have in the past, our response will be predictable. When major companies have been shown to have exploited child labour, for instance, we are instantly aggrieved and disappointed, but an understanding of the consumer mindset shows us that this is largely a cognitive dissonance response reflecting our own disappointment at having trusted the brand in the first place. Hence the PR gurus who handle the subsequent fallout employ their arcane skills in showing errant companies how they can best appeal to the consumer by means of a form of a coded apology accompanying highly publicised evidence of new, contrite and responsible behaviour.

trusted brands   Despite our burgeoning understanding of the pitfalls of aligning ourselves with *trusted brands*, we continue to accord the values we seek to individual brands and will continue to trust in these favourite brands. As competition between global brands becomes greater, we shall see further corporate agglomeration, and the similarities between brands in one sector will spill over into other sectors too. If we look at the premium pet foods available in the specialist sector, including vets and specialist pet shops, we find that four giant companies are present: Colgate Palmolive owns Hill's Pet Nutrition, Nestlé owns Purina PetCare, Proctor and Gamble owns the Iams and Eukanuba brands, and Mars Inc. owns Royal Canin, Whiskas and the Pedigree products. Each of these juggernaut companies is world famous in at least two other major product sectors, some in many more – Nestlé, for instance, has a massive interest in bottled waters as well as in confectionery and nutrition – and their style of business is consistent across these many sectors, all of which serves to support and strengthen the consumer's comfort with the brands and brand values they represent.

Recent mergers and acquisitions in the veterinary sector have taken the marketplace from one of around 400 smaller companies in the 1970s to one which is now dominated by a maximum of five major players, with a far smaller group of specialist and minor companies. At the time of writing, proposed mergers and acquisitions are leaving the employees of six companies unsure of their individual futures and countless pharmaceutical products having to change hands to ensure that no monopoly of supply will be created.

While employees might be uncertain of their future, many consumers, farmers and veterinarians will also be confused to find that a brand which everyone knows belongs to Company A is, from next Wednesday, to be sold and promoted by Company B. What happens to the brand values imbued in that particular product? Will they represent the new owner in the same way, or will Company B's approach to the market be radically different?

Efficacy is a prerequisite, but for our consumer mentality it is not in itself enough. If we disregard the brand values and the other attributes which have persuaded us to choose this product over the mass of available competitors, we soon find ourselves in a commodity marketplace where the only differences lie in price or delivery. How else, to pick just one example, could so many different pet foods, vaccines, wormers and flea treatments be successfully promoted to and through the veterinary channel?

THE PERSONAL TOUCH

personalisation

Alongside the theme of constant change runs a secondary theme of desire for *'personalisation'*. The concept of 'self', explored in earlier chapters, is present throughout all consumer behaviour and is a major driver of the way in which we, as consumers, adapt to or fashion change. The opportunity for personalisation is deliberately built into all our communication devices – laptops, PDAs and mobile phones. Whereas once we might have been content to use a Microsoft or Apple logo as a screensaver or as wallpaper on our screens, now we can view a digitally edited still frame from a video sequence shot in Australia and emailed within seconds to the UK. We can select from a score of default ring tones on our mobile phones or download our favourite song from our favourite artist or our favourite aria from our favourite opera. Indeed, we can compose our own songs on our phones and select a few bars of our own composition to personalise our communication devices. A brief train journey will reveal people's personal choices just for the ring tone on their mobile phone, with selections ranging from their children laughing, their dog barking, someone else whistling and a whole catalogue of instrumental and vocal music.

Why do we feel the need to do this? As well as our basic need to belong to some identifiable grouping, whether by joining a choral society or identifying with a football club or team, we have a need to display ourselves in a fashion which identifies our social standing, so that we can be spotted by other like-minded people. This display may take the form of dress coding: we may wish to adopt the Goth look, with its defining clothing and make-up, we may think the 'Sloane Ranger look' is what we wish to convey, or we may opt for the tracksuit and trainers look to display our sporting credentials or ambitions. We feel a need to be categorised up to a point, but within this generic approach we also recognise that it's necessary to stand out from the (smaller) crowd of like-minded people in order to attract the attention of other, more discerning participants in the marketplace.

We do this all the time, and only partly as a conscious act. In many cases the act of attracting attention has become habitual. As teenagers, we all learn to speak in a certain way because that's what our peer group demands if we are to fit in. If we choose not to fit in, we make certain adjustments to make it clear that we have chosen this path instead. Women learn the art of applying make-up at an early age, but there are few women who completely abandon their chosen style of application in favour of a new look. Most women adapt their old behaviour, unconsciously, when they embrace new products and new looks. Similarly, those men who adopt the 'Adonis persona', making heavy use of cosmetics and skin cleansing products, do so at an early age and then maintain their chosen level of usage throughout their lives, as this attention to their looks becomes habitual. Of course, this pleases the cosmetics companies, whose sales of male toiletries surged from £431.5 million to £580.4 million between 1995 and 1999. In a symbiotic growth pattern, sales of magazines such as GQ have risen steadily, but they have been forced to change their editorial stance from that of a lad-mag to a more 'intelligent' read in order to attract the more affluent and discerning reader who is prepared to spend serious cash on such toiletries.[11]

In our quest for personalisation, we haven't suddenly become androgynous, disregarding our gender differences, because for the vast majority of consumers gender is a highly defining aspect of the sense of self. Few groups of consumers, when surveyed, show any interest in unisex brands, but many marketers need to find areas of crossover appeal, where both male and female consumers will want to buy or use the product. The automotive industry is a good case in point: a car purchase may need to pass the consumer test for both genders. In the 1980s, manufacturers such as Renault and Land Rover made a special point of designing interiors with materials and fabrics that would not appear too masculine but equally, while appealing to women, would not put off the male buyer. However much progress has been made in the emancipation of women, most males, while implicitly accepting the equality of the sexes, still believe that men are different and that the differences are both positive and defining in their individual sense of self.

What Martin *Raymond* refers to in The Tomorrow People as 'Rainbow Youth' – the third age of consumers with increasing life expectancy and the enticing combination of affluence and available time – will undoubtedly have an effect not only on British society but globally too, as improved nutrition and better living standards spread to countries which previously had not enjoyed these benefits. This generation of pensioners will be fitter, more active and more demanding than their forebears and, unlike them, will be critical of products and services which discriminate against them or are patronising towards them. This group owns three-quarters of all personal financial assets and accounts for half the discretionary spending power in developed countries, according to research published by Senioragency International, the world's first international marketing network to specialise in campaigns directed at consumers over the age of 50. Their premise rests on number of objective reasons for taking 50 as the starting age of the senior group, regardless of their widely differing circumstances. *Raymond*

Certain triggers help marketing and advertising campaigns to achieve peak levels of interest and considerably improve receptiveness to their key messages. Many factors clearly pinpoint 50 as a turning point in life, making it a convenient starting point for the so-called '*seniors marketing*' strategy: *seniors marketing*

> As an example, at 49, on average, women become grandmothers for the first time. Three years later, in general, they're in the throes of the menopause and are experiencing real physical differences in their bodies.

> At 50, the main household mortgage is either paid off or very close, and at 52, on average, their youngest children leave the nest. From now, their own parents will begin to suffer ill health and they will be faced with their eventual death. This sad news will often result in a sizeable inheritance (at 57, on average).[12]

In marketing terms, the word 'senior' is generally used to refer to the over-50s. Of course, many people over the age of 50 are unhappy to be called senior, because it has connotations of disability or retirement. As a result, marketers are careful about the terminology, tone and language they use in advertising messages, making clear distinctions between those at the younger end of the senior spectrum and those at the older end.

Japan is much further ahead than the UK or the rest of Europe in its approach to consumers within this age group, and we can expect such trends and depth of product knowledge rapidly to become global, but 'Rainbow Youth' is already responsible for 15% of all new business start-ups in the UK alone.[13] As a result, brands, whether they be products or services, which fail to take into account the needs and desires of this new and burgeoning consumer group will be at a disadvantage in tomorrow's marketplace.

REFERENCES;

1 J.D. Davidson and W. Rees-Mogg, *The Sovereign Individual*; Macmillan 1988

2 J. Bellini, Yorkshire Forward's Going Global conference, Harrogate, September 2008

3 H. Benn, 'Releasing the innovative potential of rural economies – Why the rural economy matters'; speech at the Commission for Rural Communities summit, 5 February 2009

4 J. Bellini, Going Global conference, op. cit.

5 C. Mortishead, 'If the EU buys most of Russia's oil, why must we trade in dollars?', *The Times* 22 October 2003

6 J. Bellini, Going Global conference, op. cit.

7 *Shell Global Scenarios to 2025*; Shell International Ltd in co-operation with The Institute for International Economics, Washington, USA, 2005

8 M.R. Solomon, *Consumer behaviour – buying, having and being*, 8th edition; Pearson Education, 2009

9 Ibid.

10 T. Whitehead, in the *Daily Telegraph*, 28 August 2009

11 M. Raymond, *The Tomorrow People*; FT Prentice Hall, 2003

12 Senioragency International (www.senioragency.com/a consumer force to be reckoned with) 2009

13 M. Raymond, *The Tomorrow People*, op. cit.

CHAPTER XII
What will we be able to consider 'normal'?

What will we be able to consider 'normal'?
The gestation of the new consumer

It's a big bad world
we're doing what we can
sometimes we fall on our face
before we even learn to stand
but we get back up
shake off all the dust
and take it step by step

I can fill the whole floor to the ceiling
with all the dead wrong choices I've made
and even though we try to learn
from each other's mistakes

We'll do it again (doing it again)
we'll do it again my friend (doing it again)
we'll do it again and again
till we eventually can change
the way it's always been

Plain White T's

Charles Dunstone, the founder of Carphone Warehouse, says that his business doesn't sell 'stuff' any more; it now sells connectivity, because it is now the gateway to the online marketplace. Not so long ago, a mobile phone was just that, a phone which you could carry around with you. The Swiss still refer to them as 'handy-phones'. Now, despite its essential compactness, a mobile phone is expected to deliver sharp, competitive photography, a personal organiser, a means of access to one's emails and to the World Wide Web, plus streaming TV, sports and/or weather reports, an alarm clock and probably something for getting boy scouts out of horses' hooves. My phone has many times the capability that I have to operate it and, while we're on the subject, I'd like a bigger screen, please. Now we have digital SLR cameras just as effective as the old type, but a fraction of the weight and with superb performance; we have intuitive PDAs which alert you when you save something in the wrong place; we have diesel cars capable of delivering more than 70 mpg, electric cars able to keep up with 'the real thing' but costing 20% less to run, and a government which has decided that analogue TV is no longer viable and has decreed that from a certain date it will no longer be available – at all. Quite what the 6 million of us in the UK who will be living in a digital black spot are going to do has not been announced at the time of writing, but perhaps the coverage and connectivity offered by software innovators Serena IT will be available as a personal 'cloud', ensuring not only high-speed connectivity but also customisation to meet our individual needs.

The new consumer definitely exists but it's now impossible to tell whether the world has changed to meet the needs of the new consumer or whether the new consumer is setting the agenda for the future. Things started to change at the beginning of the Industrial Revolution, which is attributed by many historians to John Kay's flying shuttle, which mechanised weaving in 1733. The reality is that it had already begun some twenty-one years earlier, when Thomas Newcomen built the first commercially successful steam engine to keep deep coalmines clear of water. This was the first significant use of a power source other than wind and water. Three years earlier still, however, Abraham Darby had used coke to smelt iron ore, replacing wood and charcoal as fuel. That was surely the start of the Industrial Revolution – wasn't it? Not if you believe George P. *Landow*, Shaw Professor of English and Digital Culture at the National University of Singapore, whose timeline[1] shows that the previous year Jethro Tull's mechanical seed sower had facilitated large-scale planting in rows (for easier cultivation between the rows) and even that, 150 years earlier again, the Reverend William Lee had invented the Stocking Frame, a mechanical device for knitting stockings. The point is that what we've spent a lifetime describing as a revolution was in fact an evolution, and a similar evolution is taking place in consumerism. However, it seems that when evolution happens very quickly we tend to call it a revolution, so maybe that is what's happening now with consumers. Certainly there has never been a time when changes in consumer behaviour were as sudden and as profound as they are now.

Ronald *Regan* is credited as saying 'I've thought a bit of the shining city on the hill' in his farewell speech to the nation.[2] Detractors might cite John F. Kennedy's reference to something similar in a speech delivered in 1961 or even its original use in John Winthrop's sermon 'A Model of Christian Charity', given in 1630. Winthrop was warning the Puritan New England colonists who

Landow

Regan

were to found the Massachusetts Bay Colony that their new community would be a 'city upon a hill', watched by the world. However we look at it, people have responded to aspirational positioning since the beginning of time and marketers have been ready and willing to harness aspiration as a key driver of behaviour.

Everyone is aspirational: every one of us aspires to something different, usually something more than we have already, and the desire to improve ourselves, either intellectually or materially, is both ingrained and endemic in the human psyche. Nevertheless, we are now at an intersection where the 'old consumer' is beginning to fall away, to be replaced by the 'new consumer', according to David Lewis and Darren Bridger in their book *The soul of the new consumer*.[3] They make two salient points: first, scarcity drives behaviour. Whereas the 'old consumer' was beset by a scarcity of cash, choice or availability, today's 'new consumers' are beset by a need for time, attention and trust. It is no longer enough to say that consumers are either cash-rich and time-poor or vice versa, because today's 'new consumer' requires something better than spin and hype to promote a service or product which is under consideration. Secondly, whereas the 'old consumer' was generally uninformed and uninvolved, the 'new consumer' is no longer conformist but can be expected to be both highly informed and independent, involved and individualistic.

THE REAL THING

In our veterinary world, we have been talking for the last decade about 'service and convenience' as the catchwords of consumer demand, but this is no longer enough either. Yesterday's consumers might have been motivated by convenience, but tomorrow's consumers are motivated by a desire for authenticity. No one wants an imitation of something desirable; everyone wants the real thing.

When petrol prices were at their highest in 2008, some pet owners began to drive to their nearest practice for routine purchases but would revert to driving past as many as six or seven other practices to reach the one they trusted and had selected for 'significant' needs, because when the animal was sick or injured convenience was not the highest motivator of choice.

For reasons which no one seems able to clarify, we in the UK seem bound to follow the trends and fashions adopted by our US cousins. One of these is the US WASP work ethic which seems to require employees to arrive very early and leave their places of work very late. I'm not sure that employers actually require this of their middle and senior management, but very few are likely to tell employees to stop doing it. As a result, the one commodity which everyone seems to have too little of is time. If we have too little time to spend on our families, our relationships, our hobbies and our interests, we can expect to see stress levels rising and people demonstrating a willingness to outsource certain activities.

Where I live, there are frequent advertisements for people to do your ironing or maintain your garden, but very few offers to paint your house or service your car. Several years ago it would have been the other way round, but now car servicing is the only thing that garages can make money from and car sales are often structured simply to ensure that regular servicing forms part of the bundle of services. Very few people find ironing a joy and, with most adults in any household seeking or holding a full- or part-time job, something has to give. Outsourced ironing services appear like manna from heaven to stressed housewives and anyone else who has to do the ironing as well as everything else. This isn't just 'convenience'; it's far more a means of making sure that everything gets done in a time-poor situation. Entrepreneurs have spotted the gap and, while it lasts, are happy to fill it with work that is probably tax free and can be done from the worker's home with minimal overheads.

When we are time-poor, our relationships suffer, as our chosen contacts are starved of attention. Few of us ever write a personal letter nowadays; instead, emails and texts are dashed off with minimal attention to detail and are preferred to the 'written word' because few if any rules or conventions apply. By encouraging this lack of attention to detail, our society has reached the point where many people find it difficult to concentrate their attention for even short periods at a time. Not only that, much of our information now comes in the form of short, highly attractive visual bites, whether on TV or on our computer or telephone screens. Advertisers have discovered that they no longer need to pay for eye-wateringly expensive peak-time TV ad bundles, because there is now a plethora of different media reaching people: not only radio and TV but also the Internet, social networking sites and telephones. In addition, with the advent of Sky+ and other competing services such as Virgin, people can record their favourite TV on a hard drive, can series link it, can scroll through the adverts and can watch it standing on their heads ten weeks later, if they so wish. Media services don't have to be customised, because individual consumers are becoming adept at doing this for themselves. Just as it's hard for governments to raise and maintain an army if they cannot collect taxation, commercial broadcasters are finding difficult to maintain a programming service where it's so easy for individual consumers to avoid the advertisements that advertisers see little value in continuing with that particular model.

As advertising becomes more focused on presenting attention-grabbing images than short stories, it feeds the 'new consumer's' desire for instant gratification. How quickly we've moved on from wanting 'the real thing' to wanting 'the real thing that works best for us'. In the 1950s, the availability of TV began a process, fuelled by the availability of credit, that enabled people to short-circuit the centuries-old requirement to save. In today's world, the desire to have anything one wants is fuelled by a succession of images showing that literally everyone else already has the object of desire. No one wants to be left behind, and so individuals are encouraged to match financial folly with the instant availability of anything from a pot-bellied pig to a Porsche to fulfil their desire to belong. Of course, not just any Porsche will do: imagine your disappointment if you bought a Boxster and were then told that only a 911 is a true Porsche. Our society has become both hedonistic in its headlong rush to purchase and consume and frighteningly selfish in its disregard for anyone else but 'self'. Product purchase is no longer enough in itself: the art is to purchase 'the real thing', and every consumer, adult or child, knows it.

Our traditional structures of family, home, faith and community have been under threat since the early twentieth century, and Lewis and Bridger point to an emerging dissatisfaction with materialism and an awakening to the need for something more spiritual to take its place. Many of us find traditional faiths to be prescriptive and uninvolving; many may also find them quite hard work, requiring more attention than they expected, and there is considerable interest in other intellectual observance models, such as Pilates, personal trainers, Yoga, martial arts and New Age beliefs. Here consumerism and spirituality can combine in a satisfying investment in the required equipment, whether that be a Yoga mat or candles and crystals. A large section of society is seeking something; the problem is that, although we are all demonstrating the same desire for fulfilment, the plethora of options not only produces a fine-meshed net of alternative activities but also panders to our desire for selfish fulfilment rather than building a community of like-minded observation. In this way, self-centred consumption is fostered and encouraged by society, and this in turn produces an expectation in the next generation which reflects this 'norm'.

What is of greatest concern here is a blurring of the line between the reality of actual life and the apparent realities of the cyber-life we are increasingly coming to regard as 'normal'. Science has produced a world where no one fears illness, because we have found a cure for most diseases. There is unfortunately a growing tendency for people to believe themselves to be so well informed that they actually understand the nuances of what they have read. This leads them to make far-reaching decisions for selfish reasons, such as eschewing the opportunity to have their children vaccinated against childhood diseases, or choosing to treat their sick pets with homeopathy alone, at the same time as rejecting conventional medicine. While the last generation of family doctors were hardly able to recognise measles because they saw it so infrequently, this is sadly no longer the case, as vaccination rates have fallen perilously low in some areas of the country.

Children are no longer forced to learn their arithmetical tables and rely on calculators both in lessons and exams; punctuation and grammatical structure are often considered things of the past; and in many homes up and down the country children scarcely know where Cardiff or Carlisle is, let alone Cairo or Caracas. The theory is that this knowledge is no longer required because it can be obtained instantaneously on screen, but in this development something is being lost.

Together with the most basic of educational conventions, other 'norms' of behaviour are also changing. The digital age has brought a new phenomenon of flirting by text. It is now commonplace to sign off a text or email with a kiss. No one supposes that it has any real meaning, but again it *Greenfield* blurs the line between reality and the cyber-world of online existence. Susan *Greenfield* describes the growing confusion over who we really are in her book *Tomorrow's People*.[4] While society is pandering to the customisation of everything, allowing individuals to tailor their own version of an experience or a purchase, there is at the same time a growing trend to homogenise society, to minimise any influences of age, gender, race, faith or background – all the things that have affected the development of us as individuals. Whereas the fact that one is black may be something to say loud and proud, to say that you are white and proud of it certainly isn't encouraged. We talk about 50 being the new 30 and 60 being the new 40 because we look so different from our parents when they attained that age, but most of us play down our age; many of us, if we haven't any recent record of religious observance, are not entirely sure about our faith; and while society is focusing a great deal

of attention on women, with huge sections of industry dedicated to producing specialist products and services for women, apart from some male grooming products there isn't the same amount of commercial energy being addressed to the joys of being male.

Intriguingly, despite the strong numerical bias towards women in veterinary practice – heavily populated by young female graduates, with an almost exclusively female nursing staff and attended by pet owners who are at least 50% female – a marketing opportunity remains which no one, to date, has filled. There is a UK home-visiting veterinary service provided by female vets and targeted at female pet owners, and one wonders whether that might prove a successful model for the future.

I remember commenting some years ago that the new phenomenon of blogging wouldn't last. Why would anyone read the self-centred ramblings of an individual who was not specially qualified to comment on the vagaries of society, I asked? What a mistake! I had no inkling at the time that, not only was I wrong, I was wrong to the tune of the billions of people who have rapidly and hungrily embraced blogging by legions of otherwise complete unknowns on Twitter or the joys of other social networking sites, such as Facebook for the general audience and Cafe Mom, Black Planet, Disaboom and Elftown (among scores of others) which link people through similar interests or shared problems. These names give a clue to the vacuous pleasure that people take in describing the hourly unfolding of their own lives, but to think that this is the only value offered by such sites is to miss the real point. In a society that is, consciously or unconsciously, seeking to find itself, with individuals torn between the need to be cool and to fit in and simultaneously faced with a set of requirements to ensure that they don't do anything uncool or attract unwelcome attention to themselves (a more powerful driver than the alternative), social networking sites give individuals the opportunity to be what they would like to be. People's Facebook pages are filled with pictures of them doing the things they want other people to see them doing. If they stumble across a celebrity, there's a high degree of probability that tomorrow's page will feature a picture of them with that celebrity, giving the impression that they meet and converse all the time.

social networking   The cyber-world of *social networking* operates on the same principle as Wikipedia: it's populated by the offerings of society as a whole and has no authoritative control mechanism. And if this is not enough, people can live cyber-lives with entirely fictional cyber-personalities, cyber-relationships and even cyber-sex. The line between gaming, where structured parameters are set into the game, and individually tailored cyber-existences has become further blurred. The problem with this blurring of the lines is that society needs to feel comfortable with where the boundaries are. Today, one in six of us meets our partner on line. This has become a legitimate, even a desirable way to carry out a courtship or romance, yet the same parameters that apply here are used to further the less desirable attentions of paedophiles and others who prey on the vulnerable or the innocent. The technology which has made online dating so easy and desirable can easily be abused by the antics of teenagers who use sexting – texting risqué pictures of themselves or others to trusted recipients. Rather too often, the providers of these images find their photography posted on the Internet for the world to see. Again, the technology is running ahead of our ability to control it.

These are straightforward examples of how space-age technology affects our daily lives with varying degrees of desirability. In what ways could it affect the veterinary practice of tomorrow? As in human medicine, we are likely to see advances in technology making possible a great number of life-preserving and life-extending techniques, many of which will be non-invasive. Even ten years ago, the option of sending a dog or cat for an MRI scan would have been considered almost science-fiction by most practices, and yet today most practices refer patients for MRI examination, and some practices even have their own MRI scanner. Just as we have forgotten how, when we wanted to make a phone call, we used to turn a dial to select the numbers and that the whole process took up to a half minute to connect us, whereas connections now are so instantaneous that we worry if it takes a nanosecond longer than we anticipated, so we now worry about the seconds that an MRI scanner make take to complete its scan. As Susan Greenfield asks, what if we could marry the instantaneous nature of magneto-encephalography (MEG) with the deep reach of fluorescent optical dyes to enable better understanding of the minute workings of individual cells? Scientists predict that, in human medicine, this should be possible using a non-invasive technique within a decade. Others, like Ray Kurzweil,[5] believe that within ten to twenty years nano-robots could be inserted into the brain or other parts of the body to give a constant readout of functionality. If our consumers believe that these things are possible in human medicine, nothing other than cost and the ethical awareness of the veterinary surgeon should stand in the way of their availability in veterinary medicine.

If veterinarians are to harness the awesome power of technological advances in medical capability, will veterinary surgeons then be required to act as moral arbiters for a society which has come to believe in limitless longevity and seems to have lost much of its reliance on an old-fashioned moral outlook? To date, we have managed to fend off the requirement to perform a kidney transplant on a cat just because the pet's owner has sufficient resources to request it. Most pet owners today are easily persuaded that it would be kinder to the animal to cease treatment, but in an increasingly selfish and affluent society this may not always be the case. A child born today won't know what it is to be without online access to all the world's information; similarly, without the robust maintenance of social and moral standards during that child's education, what would stop a generation of children demanding cats without claws and dogs without barks, simply because these 'products' might be available elsewhere?

Conversely, there is recent and welcome news that, in the USA, Banfield, The Pet Hospital, has announced that it will no longer offer tail docking, ear cropping or devocalization of dogs in its hospitals, although the veterinary hospitals will continue to offer this surgery when it is medically necessary. The decision was made by the company's internal Medical Standards Board and is in line with the policy of the American Veterinary Medical Association (AVMA), which states that these procedures should only be done for therapeutic reasons. So society has to balance medical capability with moral judgement and, by our current standards, is still capable of doing so. Perhaps tomorrow's consumers will need to be guided by tomorrow's veterinarians as to what is desirable and ethically justifiable. This is clearly already the case in the USA.

As our understand of the human genome grows, so the opportunities for development of novel vaccines and other targeted drugs increase. Many pharmaceutical companies find R&D for the whole gamut of diseases unaffordable but are concentrating on specific disease types in sometimes very tightly constrained research fields. The likelihood is that in future we shall see fewer blockbuster drugs aimed at the mass market and far more individually targeted drugs. Should this happen in animal health, we can expect informed consumers to desire and even expect these drugs to be available for their pets, even though the costs per individual are likely to be far higher. To facilitate this, pet owners will have a greatly increased need for pet insurance to offset veterinary bills, and the current reluctance among veterinary surgeons to promote pet insurance cannot be seen as an adequate response to a growing need for synergy between the profession and the insurance industry.

TOMORROW'S PEOPLE

CIA World Factbook   The *CIA World Factbook* profiles every country of the world and offers comparisons with other countries where directly comparable data are available. Interestingly, the UK has 61,113,000 inhabitants with a median age of 40.2 years but a population growth rate of only 0.279%. We rank 65th in the world for our death rate, 182nd for the live birth rate and 175th for fertility. After many years of higher immigration than emigration, 90% of our population now lives within what is defined as an 'urban' environment and the fastest-growing sector of our population is the over 90s. To sum up, our population is ageing and (if immigration is excluded) shrinking and the majority of us live in or around towns. We can expect people to live longer, women will still outlive men and, in the current economic climate, people living on savings will be less well off than they would have been before the credit crunch. Economic recovery in the UK probably won't be rapid, and artificially depressed interest rates will penalise that section of the elderly population that is dependent on investments. Some companies, such as B&Q and McDonalds, have discovered that employing the over 65s has boosted customer satisfaction and retention as well as adding to the company's bottom line. These are not typical corporate responses, but they are encouraging at a time when many employees consider themselves to be vulnerable as soon as they are over 40. We should expect normal working life to continue to the age of 70–75, but where companies set a retirement age many people will draw their pensions early to supplement less well-paid and often voluntary jobs which will take them into their early to mid 70s.

Table 12.1: *Differences in state retirement age*

Italy	both sexes 58, rising to 60 by 2013
France	both sexes 60, public sector 55 in some cases
Belgium	both sexes 60
UK	men 65 and women 60, rising to 65 for both sexes by 2020 and to 68 by 2024
USA	both sexes 67 for full benefits
Mexico	both sexes 70

Source: P. Dixon, *Futurewise, six faces of global change*; HarperCollins, 1998 (adapted)

Governments are finding it ever more difficult to fund retirement pensions as well as (where it is provided at all) healthcare. Increasingly, they are looking to 'double tax' current taxpayers to provide for existing cases where pension provision is inadequate, as well as encouraging taxpayers to make better private provision for their own healthcare and retirement (see Table 12.1).

Unfortunately, with increased longevity and a faltering commitment to a socialist approach to state benefits, we can also expect a growing elderly underclass who may be forced to choose between working at poorly paid jobs until they can no longer do so and being unemployed on minimal benefits.[6] Additionally, the failure of many pension funds to deliver the promised results had already seriously disrupted people's retirement planning long before the 2008 credit crunch. Nevertheless, however bad we may consider the UK's planning for the nation's expected longevity, it is far better than the arrangements in place in Germany, which has never fully recovered from absorbing Eastern Germany into the newly unified nation in 1990. The cost of reunification will take a further twenty years to work through the system.

Outlandish as it may seem, some forecasters have warned that we should expect the emergence of a new medical specialism linked to human happiness, a topic which is seen as a focus of this new millennium. Alongside this, we should see a rise in demand for psychiatric care, as people living in burgeoning national or regional populations respond to increasing levels of stress related to employment or financial pressures and other causes of emotional fragility. Patrick Dixon anticipates that one in five of us in the UK will require psychiatric care during the first twenty years of this century.[7]

However, those elderly members of the population who have adequate incomes are likely to want to travel and enjoy new experiences. A whole new marketing sector has sprung up to meet this need, offering products and services from bespoke travel arrangements to luxury cruises lasting several weeks at a time. New products abound for the fit and active elderly, from cosmetics to clothing and from fitness clubs to financial products.

We have seen that the older generation has become more adept at using the Internet and, while their level of usage may not compete with that of the younger generations, it is still rising fast, reflecting this age group's comparative wealth and availability of time. According to the Pew

ew Research Center's

Research Center's Internet & American Life Project surveys 2006–2008 (see Table 12.2), 25% of all adult Internet usage is by people in the age groups 45 to 73+.

Table 12.2: Online activity by age group

Online activity by	age group							
Activity, %	12-17	18-28	29-40	41-50	51-59	60-69	70+	Avg
Go online	87	84	87	79	75	54	21	72
Online games	81	54	37	29	25	25	32	36
School research		73	60	61	48	33	14	57
Instant message	75	66	52	38	42	33	25	47
Text message		60	44	29	15	11	8	35
Get info about a school	57	59	42	50	40	30	14	35
Download music	51	45	28	16	14	8	5	25
Read blogs	38	41	30	20	21	19	16	27
Download video	31	27	22	14	8	8	1	18
Create a blog	19	20	9	3	9	3	4	9
Get health info		73	84	80	84	68	72	79
Travel reservations		50	72	64	64	59	60	63
Job research		44	59	59	54	31	13	51
Use gov sites		41	56	64	60	55	45	54
Bank online		38	50	44	37	35	22	41
Religious info	26	30	38	24	28	28	28	30
Use email	89	88	92	90	94	90	89	91
Get news	76	72	76	75	70	74	68	73
Product research		79	80	83	79	74	60	78
Online purchase	43	68	69	68	67	65	41	67
Job hunting	30	62	51	40	36	17	2	44
Use a photo service		39	38	31	32	31	30	34
Rate a person or product		36	34	27	31	24	8	30
Search for a person		31	31	23	23	24	29	27
Participate in an online auction		26	29	25	20	18	6	24

Source: Pew Internet & American Life Project, 2009

The biggest increase in Internet use since 2005 has been in the age group 70–75. Just over a quarter (26%) of 70–75-year-olds were online in 2005; now 45% of them are online. Internet users aged 18–32 are the most likely to use the Internet for entertainment and for communicating with friends and family. These younger generations are significantly more likely than their elders to seek entertainment from online videos, online games and virtual worlds, and they are also more likely to download music to listen to later. Internet users aged 12–32 are more likely than older users to read other people's blogs and to write their own; they are also considerably more likely than older generations to use social networking sites and to create profiles on those sites. Younger Internet users often use personal blogs to update friends on their lives, and they use social networking sites to keep track of and communicate with friends. We can probably expect to see the various differentials in usage level out as time goes on. For now, though, young people dominate the online population (see Figure 12.1).[8]

Figure 12.1: The adult Internet population

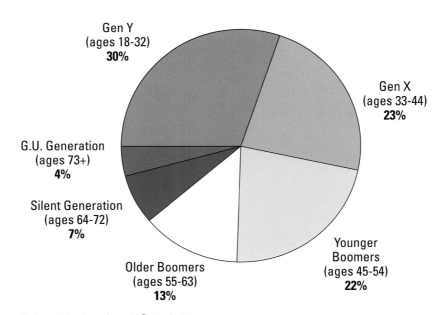

Makeup of Adult Internet Population by Generation (does not include teens)

Gen Y (ages 18-32) **30%**

Gen X (ages 33-44) **23%**

G.U. Generation (ages 73+) **4%**

Silent Generation (ages 64-72) **7%**

Older Boomers (ages 55-63) **13%**

Younger Boomers (ages 45-54) **22%**

Source: Pew Internet & American Life Project, 2009

At this other end of the scale, we have a significant number of young people still living at home, because the cost of living is too high for them to pay rent while saving a deposit to buy their own

homes. For many people, purchase is not currently an option and renting is the only alternative.

If house purchase, which has been the bastion of middle-class aspiration in the UK for the last sixty years, slips from the level of priority it enjoyed in the late 1990s, what will replace it? The explosive growth of Facebook and other social networking sites has, depending on your point of view, either facilitated or fostered the growth of personal communication and the establishment of a completely new dimension in the importance of 'self', predominantly in younger members of society. While this trend might, over time, affect a generation's ability to converse face to face rather than on line, it simultaneously generates online tribalism, whereby networkers find groups of friends or like-minded people to associate with. Already, marketers are targeting groups of like-minded networkers, using the endorsement and recommendation of leading members as leverage.

future consumers ## PET OWNERSHIP BY *FUTURE CONSUMERS*

From the point of view of pet ownership, neither end of the age curve looks encouraging. We can reasonably expect dog ownership to become more difficult, or at best less attractive, for a younger generation with no homes of their own and, in the absence of a need to plough income into housing, a more selfish and hedonistic approach to life. At the same time, fit and active retirees with several years of affluent life ahead of them may prefer the lure of freedom to travel to the comparative entrapment of pet ownership. On the other hand, with higher unemployment and reduced employment opportunities for young people, opportunistic urban crime is unlikely to fall in the near future, so people may come to see dog ownership as a creative alternative to expensive house contents insurance.

Such changes are unlikely to be gradual, however, and may be influenced by an event or trend coupled with a viral response. Cultural shifts are notoriously difficult to spot in the early stages, but those who are most connected to the trend or most influential within it find the momentum easier to identify. As our culture becomes more and more urban, the networks of those whom we either influence or are influenced by, established according to our own individual points of reference, will become more of a mini-community in themselves. In the Internet age, the first significant change to these points of influence may be their huge geographic spread, facilitated by the Internet and other electronic media. The second significant change will be the speed with which information, advice, recommendation, endorsement and prejudice will disseminate. The third will be the lightning speed with which networks overlap and multiply. The business network LinkedIn is a good example. Individuals specify contacts whom they are happy to have linked to their own page on the LinkedIn site, but each of those contacts may bring with it a hundred other business contacts, all of whom are instantly 'approved' because they are associated with a member who is respected and already 'approved'. These networks spread faster than cell multiplication and are already being targeted by marketers, who see potential in these linked relationships just as they do in the networks of like-minded 'friends' on other social networking sites.

Imagine that someone who belongs to a social networking site has bad experience in a shop.

Within minutes, that experience will have been posted on a 'wall' and transmitted at warp speed around the group. Others within the group, and with overlapping networks, will pick it up and transfer it in more than one communication plane. Within 24 hours, the viral mechanism will have done its work and the opinion of one person will have been shared, endorsed and embellished. More importantly, it will have been taken as fact and may have been accepted with little or no question by literally thousands of recipients. Whatever the background, the nuance or even the truth of the original problem, a consumer version will have been pasted on countless screens and in countless minds within a very short time. Networks operate on the basis of 'social reciprocity',[9] the implicit but rarely articulated understanding that, if I do something for you, you will do something for me. The power of networks derives from the understanding that they are only subscribed to by those who wish to belong and can therefore let certain people in while keeping other people out. There is an implicit requirement for trust, and as a consequence content – whether factual or opinionated – is accepted with minimal questioning. One can see the future for sellers of goods or services becoming far easier for those who can access these networks and far more difficult for those who cannot.

As the world's population explodes, we should expect a dramatic rise in the incidence of global pandemics. The risk of disease from new or successfully mutated viruses is both heightened and accelerated. We are seeing more and more viruses 'jump' from one species to another, and it would be reasonable to expect more of these zoonoses to develop and spread. Although we have seen a breakthrough in the availability of gene technology to counter influenza and some other viruses, we can expect some epidemics to take us by surprise.

The consumer is both empowered and hobbled by the new rapid communication systems. When avian flu was thought to be becoming a problem in 2007–08, a number of cat owners dumped their pets on farms and in other out-of-town locations, because their vision of a zoonotic spread of disease had been coloured by an ill-advised newspaper article suggesting that cats, as natural predators, would be responsible for the rapid spread of the H5N1 subtype of avian influenza. When Tamiflu first became available in the UK, several people found that it was possible to obtain the drug by lying on line and then sell it at a profit. Within just hours of this being reported on line, the practice had multiplied a hundredfold until, fortunately, the NHS website collapsed under the fearful weight of usage.

So will pet ownership end up being largely an indulgence for the rich, who can afford the pet insurance and the veterinary fees; will it be affected by other socio-economic pressures, such as employment or the availability of rented property which permits pet ownership; or will it be limited by the selfish nature of a more acquisitive and hedonistic society? Will dog ownership be encouraged by a more lawless society or hampered by far faster dissemination of the usual 'dog bites child' stories, particularly if the bitten child belongs to an influential contributor to a social networking group? Will the threat or actuality of a zoonotic pandemic reduce our willingness to share our family homes with companion animals, or will the gradual decline of our indigenous songbirds be successfully pinned on the domestic cat?

Whatever the next twenty years may bring, veterinary practice will need to serve communities of increasingly well-informed, opinionated and highly connected consumers. Good service will be rewarded with networked recommendation and poor service with rapidly networked disapprobation. Education will be more superficial and will increasingly be disseminated through websites without any process of moderation or verification.

History suggests that there will be fewer children and more older people than there are today, although recent figures published by the Office for National Statistics show that, for the first time in almost half a century, natural change (i.e. the difference between the birth and death rates) has overtaken immigration as the largest contributor to population growth. With 791,000 births in 12 months, the population of the UK rose by 408,000 to 61.4 million in the year to June 2008, the biggest annual increase since 1972.[10] However, immigrant mothers accounted for more than half of this increase in births, despite a sharp rise in the fertility of UK-born mothers. Statisticians have claimed that this indicates a desire on the part of families and single women to have children earlier in life, putting to one side the career obsession which so characterised women's attitudes in the last two decades of the twentieth century. While this may be true, and a surge in fertility would be a response to a reduction in the age of childbearing women, the larger family sizes in more recent immigrant populations and the higher dependency on state income benefits in these and second-generation immigrant populations will also affect the way society develops over the next decade.

Statisticians predict that the UK population will exceed 70 million within the next 25 years,[11] even if immigration remains at the same level. However, the figures highlight the fact that the UK population has aged, with more than 1.3 million people – one in every 50 – being aged 85 or over. In Europe alone, the number of children aged under 15 has shrunk by almost 25% since 1970 and, according to UN Populations Statistics, the number of working-age people to support every European over the age of 65 will fall from 4 to 2 by 2050.[12] Europe can only cope with this by boosting its birth rate by over 60% by 2020, which will not be possible without immigration on a previously unimaginable scale.[13] Economists recognise that, for Europe to remain economically competitive, immigration must be the norm. Of course, we also need to anticipate that, if climate change proceeds as currently expected, vast swathes of subtropical land may become uninhabitable. This would inevitably result in mass emigration from these areas to a comparatively cooler climate, which would be found in regions such as Northern Europe.

In recent months, during more straitened economic times, we have seen a net reversal of immigration from Eastern Europe as many migrant workers have returned to their native countries, where economic conditions may be more favourable. This may prove to be a see-saw motion, however, with workers from the enlarged EU picking and choosing among the more receptive member states to determine where they will work for the foreseeable future.

A snapshot of tomorrow's Britain shows rising numbers of dependent individuals in the case of younger families, higher unemployment and an increase in the elderly population. Pressure on urban living will increase, with higher levels of consumer expectation and a rise in urban stress. Within veterinary practice, employers will need to provide more family-friendly conditions for employees,

with childcare provision to retain female staff and healthcare and retirement options for all employees.

The biggest challenge for practices, however, will be to identify trends in consumer attitudes and behaviour. All trends work in the same way: new behaviours impact the status quo, which is – quietly and invisibly – receptive to change, and, by being in contact with those who share the same ideas and viewpoints, we have the opportunity to link up with them or be absorbed into their groups, networks or alliances. Whether we do that consciously or even unknowingly, our individual receptiveness and our collective awareness begins to change, so that opinions are formed and ideas accepted or rejected collectively. For centuries, we have sensed that things might change, but that change might be resisted through popular science or by falling back on cultural imperatives. Such excuses are rapidly disappearing, as science transports us individually and as a species to places we never dreamed might be possible.[14] Individual, Canute-like resistance is replaced by an understanding that there are rules governing many of these changes and a mechanism for accepting and capitalising on them.

The future belongs to those who know how to harness these social and cognitive changes and the warp speed at which they occur. Every one of us is a consumer, and as such we have a head start in understanding how other consumers think and operate. The challenge for professionals such as veterinary surgeons is on the one hand to be willing to accept change quickly enough not to be left behind, and on the other simultaneously to overlay consumer aspiration with the ethical and responsible caveats that the vocation requires. In my view, the days of resistance are over: tomorrow's consumers will want and will select those veterinary businesses that are in touch and connected to them through a number of individual and collective points of contact. This will have ramifications for the kind of staff which practices employ and for their communicative skills, and much greater ramifications for the type of investment which practices choose to make, not only in the technology of veterinary science but also in identifying and harnessing the 'buzz in the air' which others are hearing.

For generations, veterinary surgeons have been trained to use all five senses to identify the signs and signalment of injury and disease. In tomorrow's world and with tomorrow's consumers, veterinary surgeons will need, additionally, to identify and engage with the signs and signalment of changes in consumer expectation. Listening will be even more of an essential skill if practitioners are to continue to practise the art as well as the science of veterinary medicine.

REFERENCES;

1 www.victorianweb.org/technology/ir/irchron.html

2 Ronald Reagan's Farewell Address to the Nation, Oval Office, 11 January 1989

3 D. Lewis and D. Bridger, *The soul of the new consumer*; Nicholas Brealey, 2001

4 S. Greenfield. *Tomorrow's People – How 21st Century Technology is Changing the Way we Think and Feel*; Penguin, 2004

5 R. Kurzweil, *The age of spiritual machines: when computers exceed human intelligence*; Penguin, 1999

6 P. Dixon, *Futurewise, six faces of global change*; HarperCollins, 1998

7 Ibid.

8 S. Jones and S. Fox, *Generations Online in 2009*; Pew Internet & American Life Project, 2009

9 R.A. Hanneman and M. Riddle, *Introduction to social network methods*, Chapter 8; University of Northern Colorado, 2005 (online textbook: http://www.faculty.ucr.edu/~hanneman)

10 Office for National Statistics (www.statistics.gov.uk)

11 T. Whitehead, in the *Daily Telegraph*, 28 August 2009

12 UN World Population Prospects, 2008 Revision

13 M. Raymond, *The Tomorrow People*; FT Prentice Hall, 2003

14 Ibid.